FRACTURED

INTO

WHOLENESS

SUSAN H. LAWRENCE

Copyright © 2019 Susan H. Lawrence
All rights reserved.
ISBN-13: 9781096958017

Cover design by Shelby Smith
Editing by Lisa Womble (lisawomble.com)

All Scripture quotations are taken from the Holman Christian Standard Bible®, Copyright © 1999, 2000, 2002, 2003, 2009 by Holman Bible Publishers. Used by permission. Holman Christian Standard Bible®, Holman CSB®, and HCSB® are federally registered trademarks of Holman Bible Publishers.

The events recorded in this book are presented to the best of the author's ability as she experienced them, although others might have a different perspective of the same events. No harm is intended by anything shared throughout the book.

INTRODUCTION

I'm not sure I'm ready to start writing. Yet I know it's time. That seems to be a theme in the past couple years:

God, I'm not ready.

Yes, you are.

Are you sure?

Are you really asking me if I'm sure?

(Am I sure I want to respond to this question?)

If I am ready, you are ready.

Right. Here we go.

So, here we go. I trust God deeply. You might not share my faith. That's okay. I hope you won't let our differences get in the way as you read. Our beliefs and experiences might be different, but we've all gone through struggles. That's our common ground.

As we experience crises, we may feel so many different things: hurt, doubt, betrayal, fear, rejection, anger, resentment, jealousy, grief, joy, contentment, peace, faith, love, kindness, goodness, thankfulness. Our situations differ, but our experiences of them have similar feelings.

One of my favorite college courses was about group dynamics, and I learned how process is more important than content. We focus too much on content sometimes, the details of what's going on, instead of expanding our view and seeing it all in a broader context. When we choose the narrow focus, we miss appreciation, lessons, and connections.

The content is important, and I'll share many details of my experiences along the way, but don't let them get in your way if they are different from yours. Even if our situations are similar, our responses might not be. That's okay. We don't have to compare ourselves to each other. Sometimes I choose well, and sometimes I don't. I'm not always right, and I'm not always wrong. I'm learning.

My hope is you find some encouragement as I share my journey. Perhaps it will help you heal your own pain or help someone else with theirs. In order to grow, we need to learn some lessons and dig into gratitude—not just for the easy stuff of life but also for the dark depths.

Sometimes we want to focus on the tiny pieces of our lives that seem to be exploding around us. But when there are a million of those pieces flying through the air and scattered on the ground as it seems like your very life swirling around you, there is no making sense of all of the fractured pieces. It's time to find wholeness.

Blessings, Susan

THE FRACTURE

1

Ugh.

It's the first word I typed under the new note I had just opened on my phone app. I have a variety of notes in the app. One titled "shopping" so I can easily keep up with what I need at the store. Another titled "gifts" so I can make a note when someone close to me mentions a favorite that might make a good future Christmas or birthday gift. Another titled "writing ideas" that hosts a stream of odds and ends, thoughts and experiences that spur blog ideas.

But this one was titled something I never thought I'd type:

Divorce.

I didn't see it coming.

That made me feel stupid, because I'm an observant person. In fact, I probably notice more than is for my own good at times. But it's a skill that also serves me well. It helps me help others.

This time it failed me.

I came home from my annual writing retreat less than a week before, and there was definitely something bothering my husband. He was unsettled and irritable, but he didn't seem to want to share much. I gave him space, hoping he'd continue conversation in his own time. But the end of the week came, and I broke the silence.

He reluctantly and vaguely shared what seemed to me to be a disconnected stream of discontentment about his past, present, and future. Nothing was brought up about our marriage until I asked how he saw me in all of it. What I meant was, "How can I help you move forward?"

What I got was a cold stare, a dark look I had never seen from him.

It felt like several minutes passed. Maybe it was 30 seconds.

He broke the silence: *I guess that answers your question.*

No. Silence and a cold stare boring through me didn't answer my question at all. I was confused and uncomfortable. It was as if the room turned ice cold and I was sitting in front of someone I didn't know. I heard fragments of phrases:

...I deserve to be happy...

...don't want to be married...

...never been compatible...

...we've tried and failed...

...no chance...

Counseling?

No.

Talk with close friends?

No.

Some time apart?

No.

Help me understand?

No.

And that is how I found myself in the spare bedroom, opening the app on my phone and titling a note "Divorce." And I typed the first word: Ugh.

So, maybe it's not actually a word. Looking back, the fact that I could get an app open on my phone and start a new note and type three letters was a huge accomplishment.

My world seemed dark. I had never been as hurt as I was in that moment. It is because of our deep relationships with people that we feel pain and grief when there is separation, distrust, loss, and betrayal. It is the depth of the love that creates the gap when that love is withdrawn.

I'd experienced hard stuff before, but this was different. This was the person I trusted the most, the one who was home to me, the one I anticipated living the rest of my life with.

And all I felt was coldness from him.

I was alone, and I felt like I had no choice in the matter. My marriage, what I always saw as a lifetime-for-better-or-worse commitment, was shattered. A commitment that takes two was ending, and I didn't have a say in the matter. I had no choice.

Yet I did.

"I get a choice."

That's the second thing I wrote on my phone that night.

There are a lot of things I didn't get to choose about the end of my marriage, but I still had choices. I could choose how to respond. I couldn't make sense of the million pieces of my life that were swirling around me. I didn't have control over it all.

There was a time in my life when lack of control would have freaked me out. I travel and speak at events around the country, and I often admit to groups that I'm a recovering control freak. It brings some laughter and nods, because so many people get it. But I've learned control is just a mirage. We have responsibility but not control, and from the depths of the darkness that night, I chose to respond the best I could with responsibility. In the days that followed, I learned that choice was not easy. It was a choice I was forced to make over and over in the days and months and years to come.

As I sat in the dark of the spare bedroom and reeled in the swirling mess, the only thing I knew was God.

Nothing specific about Him. I couldn't think straight enough to focus on specifics. Just God.

God is.

I knew I could trust Him, and that was enough for right then. I didn't have energy to wrestle for answers. I didn't have enough focus to logically think through anything. Nothing seemed certain. Nothing seemed right. Yet there was a pinprick of light in the darkness. I couldn't explain it, and I didn't try, but I knew God was reminding me of who He is.

I knew I could trust Him, not because of where I was but because of where I'd been. I've learned it's in the calm times of our lives that we build strength and train for the tough times. It's like white water rafting.

When you're in the strong rapids, you do what you can to keep moving and survive. You don't have a lot of time to sit back and assess the situation and explore possible solutions. You are in crisis/move-forward mode. It's not a time of training. You can't suddenly become stronger, wiser, more experienced.

All of those traits are developed in times of calm. What we do in the smooth waters matters. Sometimes we just want to coast, to lie back and enjoy the ride, but we also have a lot of preparation to do. We have the opportunity to reflect on what works and what doesn't, check our equipment, practice our technique. We can coast, or we can become stronger, wiser, and more prepared.

In the dark of that first night, I didn't feel prepared. I felt as if I was drowning in one wave after another. Even months later, there were moments when I felt as if God was dragging me into deep waters. I felt as if I was drowning, as if God himself was dunking me in the swells of waves.

But I realized that was my perception, not reality. I didn't need to know how to swim well; God was holding onto me. I didn't need to overpower the waves; God controlled the waves. I didn't need to fight to breathe; God gave me breath. I didn't need to struggle; God had made me to float.

2

There was very little sleep that first night. I slept in the guest bedroom until I moved out several weeks later. I was a guest in his world. He wanted the house. He wanted the divorce. He wanted life with someone else. He wanted...

Before closing myself in the guest room that first night, I briefly left the house. It was after midnight, but I needed air. I got in the van and drove. I didn't know where to go, but as I got five to ten minutes down the road, I realized where I was going—or rather, *why* I was going. I wanted him to chase me, to want me enough that he would be concerned about me driving into the middle of the night.

But he didn't. And I knew there was little I could do in the middle of the night. I returned to what was my house, too, for the time. It might not be my home, because I was certainly no longer wanted or comfortable there. But I could still be there, despite what he wanted.

And what *did* he want? It felt as if his life exploded, sending shrapnel straight through me—leaving gaping, bloody wounds—as well as into family, friends, and others. In reality, it was more of an *im*plosion with such force that the range and reach of the damage was unpredictable.

I don't know where that Friday ended and Saturday began. It was dark and confusing. It was excruciating and devastating. I texted two friends I could trust and whom I knew would pray the words I couldn't. And I read Ephesians 5 (verses 10-20):

> *Finally, be strengthened by the Lord and by His vast strength. Put on the full armor of God so that you can stand against the tactics of the Devil. For our battle is not against flesh and blood, but against the rulers, against the authorities, against*

the world powers of this darkness, against the spiritual forces of evil in the heavens. This is why you must take up the full armor of God, so that you may be able to resist in the evil day, and having prepared everything, to take your stand. Stand, therefore,

> *with truth like a belt around your waist,*
> *righteousness like armor on your chest,*
> *and your feet sandaled with readiness*
> *for the gospel of peace.*
> *In every situation take the shield of faith,*
> *and with it you will be able to extinguish*
> *all the flaming arrows of the evil one.*
> *Take the helmet of salvation,*
> *and the sword of the Spirit,*
> *which is God's word.*

Pray at all times in the Spirit with every prayer and request, and stay alert in this with all perseverance and intercession for all the saints. Pray also for me, that the message may be given to me when I open my mouth to make known with boldness the mystery of the gospel. For this I am an ambassador in chains. Pray that I might be bold enough in Him to speak as I should.

I could barely focus for more than a few words. Nothing made sense. The room was spinning. So was my life.

I refocused and started to read aloud. I struggled to form words, yet I could eek out a few at a time. If I felt as if I was reading without claiming the words, truths, and promises, I stopped and backed up. I probably restarted several dozen times. But I got through it. It was months before I would attempt to get out of bed without proclaiming those words. I knew my own strength, wisdom, courage, and protection weren't enough. To get through a day—or even to get out of bed—it was only God. Only He knew all the pieces of the rubble. Only He could make me whole.

As I lay in the dark that first night, my mind swirling yet trying to focus on the immediate choices I had, I felt the consuming darkness that seeped into and surrounded me. I knew I needed to trust what I'd learned in the light while I was surrounded by the disorienting darkness.

Even though I was in the dark, I could make a decision based on the light. That's an important lesson I had learned through the years, but I never had to apply it with the fervor of that moment. Decisions made without the light of day and the light of life send horrible ripple effects through our lives and others' lives, no matter how much we choose to believe and rationalize otherwise.

I was frightened by the darkness around me that night and in the days and nights that followed, but I was also empowered by the light that pierced it.

I chose to acknowledge the reality of being surrounded by darkness, yet also remind myself I had access to the light. Moving in that direction was humbling and hard. I wanted to curl up, cover up, and give up. In the months that followed, I experienced what I knew to be true: living in the light examined and exposed me. And that's a good thing. The choices I faced weren't easy, but I could tell the good from the bad and the best from the good.

As the sun rose that first morning and I saw the light outside the window and the light in those verses about God's protection and provision, I was ready to get out of bed. But I didn't want to be in that house. It was cold. It felt empty. I needed help.

I went to a couple's house, friends to both me and my ex. These were people I knew would seek and claim truth instead of nonchalantly consoling, placating, blaming, or fixing. They were authentic, and they were crushed. They were love to me that Saturday morning. Nothing changed from the beginning to the end of our conversation. The world still seemed dark, but I opened up and they listened. Their own lives would be impacted, too. The shards continued to fly and pierce.

I will never forget the looks on their faces. I wondered what mine must have looked like when my ex delivered the news to me. The mess on my face couldn't have completely reflected the monumental mess in my heart.

My friends' teen daughter came into the house. She and I had become good friends and she had never seen me in such a mess. To be honest, neither had I. I couldn't tell her. I wasn't ready. She just walked up to me and hugged me. I cried. She stepped back and, through the tears in her own eyes, comforted me with the news: "*Finding Dory* is on Netflix!"

I laughed. I hardly recognized the sound. She was serious about trying to find something that would surely help me feel better. It is one of the sweet memories among the rubble. Kindness doesn't have to fix someone or something—it rarely can—but it gives a boost. It's a ray of hope. It's a reality check.

Months later, we had a *Finding Dory* movie night with ice cream, which was added as another "maybe this will help" ingredient. I hadn't watched a full movie since the chaos began, and it was hard to sit in leisure when so much was still swirling around me. But I loved the thoughtfulness behind the movie night, providing me a reprieve. At the end, she asked the inevitable question, "Well, did it help?"

"No, not really." But I appreciated the thought, friendship, and time.

So, I guess it actually *did* help.

3

Four friends now knew. They were obviously friends I trusted.

When I was young, trust centered around privacy. Could I trust my friend not to tell what I shared?

I've learned privacy and secrecy are different. When we want something kept quiet based on embarrassment, shame, fear, pride, or discomfort, we want secrecy. We don't want anyone to know. The process and outcome of keeping secrets are nearly always destructive.

Privacy, on the other hand, is based in respect. It sheds light in appropriate ways. It always invites transparency, truthfulness, and accountability. It never hides. It invites and reveals. It might not be widely public, but it is not hidden. And when we trust someone or someone trusts us, we will keep some things private out of respect but will not keep secrets that need to be brought into the light of truth.

That's the trust I had (and have) with those four friends in those first few hours and as time went by and more details were revealed. I knew my friends would respect my privacy but would not allow unhealthy secrets. I trusted them to seek truth and to hold me accountable. To stick with me through the long haul. To ask difficult questions and not be content with pat responses.

I didn't have the energy to sugarcoat anything.

So many pieces sped around me that I could only focus on the core of what was stable. My friends helped me with that. They reiterated the truth I knew but was struggling to hold. They were struggling and hurting, too. But they put me ahead of themselves. More importantly, they put God ahead of us all.

In addition to those close friends, I needed to tell my mom.

I texted her, "Are you home?"

"Yes."

"I'm on my way."

"This can't be good."

No. It isn't.

.....

I grew up 45 minutes from where I now live. I was the seventh generation on the family farm. Although I've lived away from my hometown nearly twice as long as I lived in it, I will always hold it dear. I grew up in a close-knit community, and that camaraderie is still important to me—now, in a different town. It is partly what motivates me to be involved in community, helping others, investing together.

I enjoyed so many things about my childhood. To me, growing up on the family farm was adventurous. My parents held us responsible. They had expectations, but they also gave us freedom. My imagination soared. I loved working and problem-solving alongside my dad. I loved being my mom's helper. I enjoyed life. My parents and my family weren't perfect— no one is—but we lived life well together.

In the deepest hurt of my life, I needed to see my mom. Not to escape, not to be coddled, but to do life together—even the stinky bowels of it.

It's not like doing the stink of life together was foreign to us. My dad died one year earlier after battling melanoma for years. The end of his life was tough, yet his attitude and my mom's commitment made the process a part of life, not something which consumed us. They were determined to find joy among the trials. They had practice through the years. They were high school sweethearts who grew through life together while letting each other grow individually. They drove each other nutty and made each other laugh. They showed me how to love well and authentically, how to sacrifice for a life partner, how to keep commitments and fight for resolution, how to take responsibility and apologize, how to invest in friends and community, how to share life generously with others.

My mom and I have a good friendship. My dad and I were buddies. Losing him was tough. I was at peace with his death, partly because of my faith and partly because of the brief but honest conversations we had as his life neared an end. But I missed him. Grief is a process, and I was still grieving when my ex set me aside.

I lost my two favorite men within a little more than one year. I had peace that my dad loved me well. He gave me a firm foundation. Even firmer was the foundation of God's love for me. I knew my identity was not in what my thought-to-be-life-partner did to or thought of me. My identity was deeper, more solid.

Devastation does not destroy truth, but devastation often makes it difficult to see truth.

I have found devastation can be strangely clarifying.

.....

I don't remember much about my 45-minute drive to my mom's that morning. I felt as if I was in a disorienting fog. I was emotionally bruised and sore. But I remember the sun was shining. I didn't have to think much about driving, because I knew the way well. It was yet another reminder of how the habits we form in the clarity of light guide us in the darkness.

I walked inside my childhood home and fell into my mom's arms. She wept for and with me before I said a word. When I got words to come out to tell her what was happening, she was shocked. The look on her face was pained. Seeing her face prompted a thought I never thought I'd have. It was the one and only time I have been grateful my dad was not alive. I wish he was here to support mom through it, but I'm glad he was spared seeing me in the worst pain of my life.

Mom and I struggled through the tears. I had no concrete explanation. It seemed so odd to relay the facts that the man who was a mental health professional and had helped so many others and had gone to counseling with me years ago wasn't open to counseling with a professional or friends. That the man of faith who had stood firmly in God's truth, wrestled with others through times of doubt, and encouraged others to choose humility and accountability now rejected an association with God. The things he would normally have done were thrown aside. I began to realize the rejection of me, our marriage, our family was a by-product. His rejection was much bigger, deeper, darker.

I don't know how much time passed as mom and I sat at the kitchen table, but I remember a lull. Then she said, "You know I have to ask, 'Did you do something?'"

I think I said something like, "Well, I'm sure I'm difficult to live with. Aren't we all? And I have certainly struggled with my own stuff that impacted our marriage years ago, but that's been 15 years ago. We worked through stuff. I have fought to get to a healthy place. I'm not perfect, but I haven't done anything that would spur this. And he said it was him and not me."

It was a brief part of our conversation that morning. But it is one of the parts I best remember. It makes me chuckle as I think back. Some might hear those words from a parent and feel blame or shame. I knew that wasn't my mom's motivation. I didn't grow up in an let's-just-sweep-the-mess-under-the-rug family. We don't pretend issues don't exist. We don't pretend people haven't done wrong. We don't shy away from confrontation—perhaps to a fault at times. We tend to ask the tough questions, deal with the fallout, respect each other's space but check in when appropriate, then continue life together.

Truth matters, and when we don't seek truth in the lives of the people we love, we can't help them and do life well with them. When we shove things under the rug, we might know where the lumps are and avoid them, but we cause others to stumble. When I hear a person close to someone who is struggling say things like, "I don't really know what's going on," and it's because they haven't asked out of genuine concern, I flinch. I know it's hard to confront the people we love, but the short-term discomfort is better than the long-term dysfunction. Dishonesty and deception come in all forms, including a polite smile and flippant "How are you?" Avoiding confrontation is not worth the cost of losing respect and relationships. Avoiding confrontation only prompts hurt feelings to become deeper, problems to become more complex, and conversations to become more difficult.

I love my mom for asking me that direct question, for opening that door, not for blame but for accountability. It was an invitation to honestly share and bring things to light, to avoid remnants of darkness.

Get it out, share, wrestle, heal. Otherwise, what's kept in the dark grows into rank crud. In the light, it shrinks. In the light, truth and lies are easier to discern. In the dark, we can't fully use our senses to determine which is which.

Darkness is disorienting.

Light is revealing.

4

I stood on a precipice. At least, that's how it felt.

It had been nearly three weeks since my ex announced he deserved a different life and refused to identify and address issues or put forth effort to work through stuff. It had been nearly three weeks since the pieces of life began to violently swirl around me. Not much of the dust had settled. I wondered if it ever could when I wasn't given the chance to identify the pieces, gain insight into what was happening, be told the truth.

But I began to realize that even the person creating the mayhem might not be in a position to identify or be transparent about the truth.

Within those three weeks, I managed to uncover the truth about some things. I vehemently sought truth, sifted for truth, reminded myself of truth, and clung to truth. It was exhausting but it was also the only healthy way I knew to deal with the destruction and to survive.

There was a suffocating heaviness in the house. I felt smothered by something I couldn't always identify, but it was disorienting. It was chilling. It was frightening. It was unsafe.

When I woke up one Sunday morning, I felt the desperate need to plant my heart firmly on truth. Right in the middle of the house. I left the isolation of the spare bedroom and sat at the dining room table. I opened my Bible, turned on worship music, and dug in. I read, journaled, and claimed truth. I emptied myself to let God fill me up, and all the while, I was keenly aware of the scoffs muttered by my ex each time he walked through the room. I felt as if I was sitting in the middle of a battlefield. It was disorienting, and I tried to stay focused, but I felt surrounded by a barrage. I sobbed as I tried to give it all to God until it was time to get ready for church.

When I returned a couple hours later, the oppressive battle I felt in that house had magnified, as if being close to God through worship made me realize the reality of how dark that house now was. It was deafening and disturbing. I looked at my ex, sitting on the couch, appearing relaxed and content. Until he looked up at me. There was the coldness again. Maybe it wasn't simple coldness. It seemed more personal than that, offensive more than aloof. When I asked how he could look at me that way after spending two and a half decades together, he shrugged his shoulders with dismissiveness, and something in me broke loose.

.....

Many years before, when on a family vacation, my dad decided to take a scenic route. It wasn't unusual. He liked to explore lightly-traveled roads. We were in the mountains, so getting away from the hubbub would certainly reveal magnificent views, and it did. But it also put us on a very narrow road on the side of a mountain. There wasn't room for two cars to pass in many places, and we met a car in just the wrong spot. Dad decided to back up to find a few extra inches to let the other vehicle by. To say it was frightening is an understatement. We were in the middle of a beautiful location, but we were also one slip away from tumbling to our deaths. It was dizzying.

.....

In the wake of my ex's cold stare and dismissiveness, I felt as if I was on a precipice. I felt surrounded by evil in a way that frightened me. I fought back in ways that alarmed me. I yelled and cursed at my ex. I used words I had learned on the elementary school bus but hadn't thought about for years. And for a while, in a way, it felt good. But I also felt as if I was too close to the edge, as if I was losing a battle, that I was yielding to a horribleness I didn't want to be a part of. It wasn't my actual words—to be honest, they were pretty lame by many standards and habits—it was the push-me-pull-me of the evil in the room. I was standing on the edge of the precipice, and I felt as if I was about to jump, that I had wiggled myself onto the ledge and left God somewhere I couldn't get back to.

At some point, I took a breath, and when I paused, I heard my ex say he deserved every word of what I'd said...then announce that he needed to go to the hardware store as he left the room.

What?

I stood alone in the house, and I was in a bad place. I felt completely disoriented, yet I was sure of one thing: I couldn't take the next step by myself. I didn't trust myself. I couldn't tell if I was going to go off the edge. I called my mom, and she wisely told me to pack a bag and get out. I fought for air as I somehow put everything I might immediately need in a bag. I took my laptop, the beginnings of legal paperwork, financial papers, identification, chargers, a couple sets of clothes, toiletries, my Bible, and Polar Pop, the small stuffed polar bear that had traveled the world with me. And I left.

I couldn't go to my mom's house. I needed to be farther away, and I needed to be somewhere my ex wouldn't try to contact me. Not that I believed he wanted to pursue me, but I needed to drive far enough away to feel safe. And driving has always relaxed me.

I am a firm believer in not running away from things. I believe it is important to know where you are running *to* and not simply run *from* something; otherwise, you don't really know where you'll end up. I could end up running straight off that cliff.

I felt as if I was fleeing for my life. Not my physical life. I wasn't in that kind of danger, but my emotional and spiritual safety were threatened. I had felt the oppression of evil, and it was dark and terrifying.

It wasn't long before I knew where I was going. I called one of my sisters, and she and her husband didn't hesitate to provide a place for me to retreat. It was a good drive. And I mean good in the not-easy-at-all way. I fought the whole way. I screamed and cried. I wrestled with God. Had I let evil get too close to me? Had I stepped away from God into a vulnerable place? Had I crossed a line?

I felt as if I had put myself on that precipice. As I struggled with that image, God soon gave me a snapshot of the reality of the situation. I was reminded once again, as I have been reminded many times since, that my perspective was incomplete, and my feelings weren't always accurate indicators or truth.

.....

I remember my dad sitting in his chair when I was little, relaxing after a long, hard day on the farm or one of his many other jobs. But he was attentive, even if it was in a nonchalant way. Sometimes I'd walk by his chair, and he'd catch my back belt loop at just the right time. I'd keep walking and feel the tension. I'd lean forward, nearly tipping over, and dad would hold firmly to me. There was only so far I could go when he held on. I giggled as I leaned forward, knowing and trusting his strength.

.....

I was indeed standing on a precipice. I had leaned over the edge and been dangerously close to careening into the depths below. I felt the imminent doom. It was as if the deadly depths of what was below me reached up to lure me. I couldn't see the bottom, but I knew the deceptive and chilling fog hid dangers from which I might never recover.

Yet I suddenly realized I wasn't in as much danger as I felt.

God held my belt loop.

I knew and trusted His strength.

He let me get that close for a reason, and He did it within His protection.

He knew exactly where I had been, where I was, and where I was headed. After all, it wasn't my fight anyway. It was bigger than me. It was His. Sure, I had responsibility in the battle. I couldn't just sit back and pretend nothing was happening. But I didn't have to figure it out. I had to keep my eyes on Him, which was often easier said than done.

It wouldn't be the last time I felt oppressed and disoriented, but it was the last time I felt that close to the depth of evil waiting to swallow me whole.

I slept in another state that night. When I left the house in Illinois, I didn't know when I'd return. I didn't know my next steps. But I woke up with strength. I didn't have all the answers, but I had the one that mattered. God wanted me to do it all His way. I knew that wasn't going to be the easy way. I knew I had a million-plus choices ahead of me, but in each one, I could choose Him. Whatever that entailed. Even when it was confusing and difficult.

I had leaned into Him that very first night of the explosion, and I now trusted Him even more. He held my belt loop when I thought I was going over the edge.

I threw my legs over the bed, and my feet were firmly planted. I packed up, appeased my sister and her husband by eating a few bites for breakfast, then I headed back. I wasn't going to run. I was going to move forward. By the time my several-hour drive was done, I had secured a house to rent, friends had delivered boxes to the house that was no longer a safe place to me, and people were putting together the moving team for that weekend. When my ex got home from work, I had already stacked dozens of packed boxes. I told him he would be paying for my rent until the divorce was final and asked him to be gone during the moving process that weekend. He agreed.

5

It's intriguing and unsettling how marriage takes two people to agree in order to make it happen, but divorce only takes one. Even when a third person is involved because of an affair, the decision to stay committed to or leave the marriage is ultimately made by a person in the marriage.

.....

Marriage begins by imagining what we want life to look like together. Then it becomes real, and we leave the fantasy behind. It's hard sometimes, but we can choose to say *I do* again and again and again. It's messy sometimes, but choosing *I do* when it's hard and messy is one of the things that makes it deeply valuable. Saying *I do* makes the sacrifices worthwhile, because we commit to togetherness. We commit to teamwork. Until someone says *I don't*. And either person can say it at any time, even when you least expect it, even when you've been intentionally saying *I do*. Those two words have ripple effects across many lives, whether it's *I do* or *I don't*.

.....

When my ex's *I do* became an *I don't*, I never really blamed the other woman. In fact, I don't like that term. She's not an "other" woman. She's another woman.

Yes, she's an adult.

Yes, she was aware I was in the picture.

Yes, she could have walked away from him.

But my ex was an adult.

He was definitely aware I was in the picture.

He could have walked away from her.

Blame and responsibility are related but inherently different. Much of the time, blame isn't helpful. Yet not assigning blame never takes away

24

the responsibility, and we can take responsibility without playing a blame and shame game.

I never wanted my ex to be blamed and shamed, but I wanted him to take responsibility. Not as much for my sake as for his. Taking responsibility requires humility and honesty, and sometimes people create a false reality that makes a situation more palatable and shifts responsibility. This process is costly to both self and relationships.

Although several people told me they believed my ex had a girlfriend, I didn't have proof, and he wasn't being honest about it. I really didn't have much energy to explore the possibility. Barely able to process what was happening on a very basic level, I'm not sure I really wanted to know more. But after a couple weeks, while I was still living in the house, I saw too many warning signs to ignore. I felt as if God tenderly peeled back just a few layers of veneer, not enough to overwhelm me, but enough that would make me open my eyes and decide to search a bit.

It didn't take long before I stared at a pile of pages that listed hundreds of conversations, going back several months, including moments I would have considered sacred to our marriage and family. I learned he was connecting with her throughout our family Christmas with our girls, Christmas with his family. Now that oddly-timed long walk he took by himself in the middle of my family's Christmas made more sense. I also saw he had been texting her intermittently during the same timeframe he was telling me he wanted a divorce. I stared at all that proof on pages and pages, and I wept.

I texted two friends who called me immediately and let me fall apart. After listening, then crying and praying with me, one said, "Susan, step away from that pile of papers. You know the truth now. How much more do you really need or want to know? Take the next step forward by discerning what God wants you to do."

Deep breath.

Yes. She was right. There was no reason to torture myself. I knew enough.

I decided not to confront my ex right away. I knew it would be with too much anger. Not that anger isn't justified at times, but if I was going to yield to God and handle this the way He intended, I needed to respond in His timing. A few days later, it was time. I didn't want to put my ex on the defense, and I knew I needed to stay calm. I needed to allow space, to be able to see the conversation as a step forward instead of a deep hole of betrayal and resentment. I didn't want to attack him; I wanted to know the truth.

When my ex got home from work, I mentioned wanting to talk with him when he had time sometime that evening. No hurry. When he said he was ready, I simply said, "I'd like to talk about your girlfriend."

He was livid. I listened to him yell about how no one knew, how did I find out, it wasn't any of my business, the divorce had nothing to do with her, no one needed to know, and so on. I responded very little. I felt remarkably calm, and I let him reveal many details I didn't yet know.

When he tried to make me feel better by saying something like, "Don't worry. She's just normal like you," I wanted to throw up or throw something, glimpsing his cluelessness as to the dynamics of what was happening. As disgusting as the situation felt, I almost chuckled at his ill-fitted attempt at reassurance.

Who was this standing in front of me?

The conversation was upsetting but also clarifying. I still couldn't understand it all, but I saw more pieces. With more pieces came more confusion. It was an odd juxtaposition. God had peeled back more veneer, and He continually reminded me of the importance of revealing truth.

Just because my ex wanted to keep it all a secret didn't mean I had to. I knew I couldn't. I would keep the circle tight for the sake of privacy, but secrecy would be too costly. It already had been. I wasn't going to leave deception in the dark any longer. He had been choosing what to hide from others and himself, but I needed to bring everything into the light. Years earlier, I had struggled with my own, different brand of deception, but it was deception just the same. I had fought for transparency in my life. It was a journey worth the effort. I wasn't going back. Living transparently had become a daily choice. Even though it was challenging at times, it brought freedom and authentic relationships with others and God.

Some people encourage honesty in your life. Others try to force it by hovering or accusing in a way that drives you back, making you feel trapped, as if there isn't an option to step into the light safely. I didn't want to be that person. I'd been on the receiving end of those accusations, and it's damaging. I tried to leave the door open for my ex to share what he needed to share in order to move forward. As hurt as I was, I still wanted to leave him in as healthy a place as possible.

Bitterness wasn't going to help either of us move forward.

As I encouraged him to make sure he was in a good place, I emphasized how important his health—emotional, relational, and spiritual—was to anyone he was going to be in a relationship with, including his girlfriend. It's hard enough to start a new relationship, let alone when it's grounded in a difficult, tumultuous situation. Deception at the beginning of a relationship doesn't invite honesty into it, no matter how "real" you think you're being with the new person. It might feel fresher than what you've had, but you're immediately adding the baggage of compartmentalizing the new person from the remainder of your life, filtering what you want him or her to know. It's not a good foundation.

If my ex was going to anticipate a life with someone other than me, I didn't want him to set himself up for failure because of the impact that would have on him, our daughters, and the girlfriend. It's hard enough to deal with the ending of a 25+ year marriage, and the grief that comes with that collapse takes time to untwist and process.

I asked him to consider the message it would send to his girlfriend if he continued to compartmentalize his life and refused to tell people about her. How could he honestly say he'd given everything he had for the new relationship when he wasn't willing to share her with anyone who had been important in his life? What message would that send to her, and what message would that send about her to others? If I was her, I'd want to know more about his life than just what he wanted to share. But then again, perhaps people only want the pieces of information that allow them to assemble a picture of reality which affirms their decisions.

Honesty and transparency matter.

I offered to talk with his girlfriend, because I wanted her to catch a glimpse of another perspective. I wanted to let her know I was a real, live person. I wanted to plant the seed of peace in case we'd ever be at family gatherings together in the future. My ex said talking to her wasn't an option. I'm not sure how I would have actually handled it if she had been willing to talk. Because of the searching I'd done, I had her phone number. Months later, when I believed it was the right time with the right motivation, I sent her a text, "Hi. I wanted to reach out to simply say I forgive you.—Susan"

It's okay that I didn't get a response. Communicating my forgiveness was important to me, and I made that effort. When my ex and his girlfriend eventually called it quits, I let him know I was sorry he was having to deal with two breakups within a year. I meant it. It was hard enough for me to cope with a destroyed marriage after two and a half decades. I couldn't imagine trying to simultaneously start a new relationship, then have it unravel, too.

I know it may seem strange to think I could actually feel this kind of empathy for my ex, and even his girlfriend, but I was trying to handle things in a way that was pleasing to God. And, interestingly enough, doing things as I felt He directed helped me to let go. On a practical level, I let go of the stack of documents that revealed the communications and relationship. A few weeks after finding out about his girlfriend, I placed it all in large manila envelope and handed it to my ex after a mediation appointment. I needed it out of my hands and heart before it took root and turned into bitterness and resentment. I included a letter of forgiveness in order to release him as well as me. Forgiveness is a process, a continual choice, and it is worth the sacrifice. If you can forgive in a tangible way, I recommend it. I didn't need to hang onto those pages. I no longer needed proof. I knew the truth. I dealt with it and continue to deal with it in as healthy a way as I can manage. With each step of release, humility, and forgiveness, I give a bit of myself to God. In response, He replaces pieces of me with His strength and wisdom.

And I sigh with some gratitude with each step.

6

Packing week was a whirlwind. It was as if I was floundering in the eye of a hurricane. I had peace, knowing I was doing what needed to be done, yet danger and destruction were so close at all times, it seemed as though I could reach out and touch them. My ex went through his routine as if nothing out of the ordinary was happening.

My new landlords rushed to prepare what I came to call my safehouse. They were gentle and gracious to me, and I was able to get into the house a couple days early to clean and prep a few things. Several people were with me, including one of my best friends. I walked through the house and suddenly felt a wave of grief. I was thankful for my safehouse, but I was deeply saddened by the need for it. Once again, a wave of "what on earth is going on" slammed against me, and I wept.

I somehow packed half of a huge house in four days and had organized piles of furniture, boxes, and tubs when the moving crew arrived that Friday night. The crew was mutual friends but mainly guys my ex had poured into through the years. It was difficult to see the pain and confusion on their faces. They didn't necessarily know what to do about the divorce, but moving my belongings gave them a productive focus. They were perplexed and angry at how a friend and mentor treated me and them; they wondered why he couldn't take the same advice he had given to them and so many others through the years. They felt rejected. So they did what they could; they carried boxes, packed their trucks and trailers, and drove back and forth across town.

Not only did we complete what was planned for Friday, but we also moved all but one thing we had planned to move Saturday. Friends prepared a meal and had it ready at my new home, and we all hung out and tried to breathe. It was an odd juxtaposition of a situation shared among friends. Tears still fill my eyes as I think about the love lived out that night and weekend. I was deeply grateful.

We had only one more item to move the next morning: my dog's pen, which was a large, heavy structure. My dad had built it with my ex and my youngest daughter before we got Della, our chocolate lab. Now my chocolate lab.

.....

We had one dog the entire time the girls were growing up, and he died during my oldest daughter's sophomore year of college. We knew we'd get another dog and started looking about a year later. We chose Della when she was only one week old and picked her up a few weeks before my youngest graduated from high school. She quickly settled into our family.

My ex often sat in an Adirondack chair in the backyard with a book or beer in one hand, and his other hand reaching over the arm to pet Della. He helped her learn to sit and catch. He talked with her and spoiled her.

When we moved to a large house in a new town several months before he ended the marriage, he was concerned about her new space, wanting to make it secure and comfortable. Pretty much any time he was on the back deck, Della was with him. Perhaps that's why I was so surprised when he wanted to give her away.

The weekend my ex told me he wanted out of the marriage, we had brief exchanges about several decisions we'd have to make, including who would live where. Because he would be staying in the big house, and we'd only recently moved, I didn't want Della to make one more adjustment. I would miss her horribly. We were buddies, and I was the one who usually fed and walked her. But she was going to have to adjust to something, and I thought it better to adjust to not having me around than to living in another new place. I also thought it would be good for my ex to have someone to hang out with him and comfort him through the transition. So, I said she could stay with him.

When he came home after work that Monday, not even 72 hours after delivering the devastating news, he yelled up the stairs to let me know he'd talked to one of his buddies, thinking he could give Della a good new home with him, but unfortunately, he wouldn't be able to take her.

What?

I was glad he could not see my face at the time. I took a deep breath and went to the top of the stairs.

You were going to give away Della?

Yes. You said you didn't want her.

I said no such thing. I said I thought it was best for her to stay here and have some stability. You are not giving her away. I am taking her.

That's fine. I don't want her.

I stood at the top of the stairs for a moment while he walked away. I was continually surprised at his dismissiveness of what was once important to him.

Maybe it was for the best. I could love on Della through the transition.

In the months to come, I realized I needed her more than she needed me. She settled into her new home quickly but was protective of me for a while. I think she sensed when I was on more stable ground, and she relaxed her guard duty a bit. She settled back into primarily wanting play and romp time.

On the Friday night of the move, we decided not to try to move Della and her house. It was going to take several strong men and a trailer, so it was best to wait until the next morning. That was okay. I had things to do that Friday night.

After everyone left my new home, I returned to the big house.

No matter how I was being treated, no matter how disrespectfully I was being pushed out of my ex's life, I was determined to extend compassion and grace. It wasn't an easy choice. I didn't do it out of some natural goodness in my heart. I continued to struggle with making the next best choice. I knew it was better to pull up the small sprouts of anger and bitterness when they first appeared than let them take deep root and create a tangled mess.

I cleaned the big house with loving care. I prayed as I scrubbed every corner of the floors, dusted what furniture my ex wanted to keep, and cleaned the piano that had brought us both so much joy through the years. I wiped cabinets and countertops I knew he'd touch often. It was my way of loving and leaving well. That's the commitment I'd made—for better or worse. This was the "worse" part. And it was a test to see how I would respond. Regardless of how hateful he was toward me, even if he chose to reject me and walk away, I could choose a different response. Because of his choices, I might not be able to stay committed to him within the marriage, but I could still fulfill my commitment to pour into him in the few ways left.

So, I cleaned and I prayed.

I slept in the bed we had shared for years. I hadn't slept in it since that first explosive night, but I settled in and prayed for him. I prayed for the person who might share that bed with him one day. I prayed for his relationship with God.

And I wept.

It might have been easier to rip apart that bed, to lash out against the woman who was vying for the space I once lived in well, to take what I wanted and leave everything else in disarray. It's not that I'm not capable of those things. I just didn't want to leave that way. Maybe I didn't have the energy to respond in those ways. Maybe I knew everything was messy enough, and I didn't want more baggage. Maybe I knew my girls were watching my treatment of their dad. I couldn't process my reasons, but I knew I could walk away knowing I had extended God's grace and kept my dignity.

Before the guys came to move Della's pen the next morning, I had written and tucked notes throughout the house, where my ex would find them in the days to come. I had already left him several notes here and there—things I wanted him to know but was certain he couldn't accept from me at the time. I hoped he could see truth and hope, even if he no longer saw it in his faith or marriage.

.....

I want you to know that I hurt for you and I am sorry that you have gotten into such a pit that you think that this is the only way out, to leave behind a relationship that you've worked on and committed to for so many years. I think I know you better than most, and I know I love you more than most. No matter what.

·····

I love you. Sure, I wish you had given me some options along the way, spoken up, been honest with me, let me try, help, comfort, apologize, etc. But neither of us can go back. Even as our marriage ends, I want to be as available as I am emotionally able to be for you. I may not have made the best choices all the time, but I am trying to, moving forward. At some point, that choice will likely be signing a piece of paper and watching you walk away. And then my choices won't affect you. But there are a lot of good choices I can make between now and then.

·····

No matter what, I hope you can accept that I love you. That you are worthy. That you bring joy to me and to others. Thank you.

·····

I haven't looked you in the eyes enough for extended periods of time lately. For that, I apologize.

·····

Sometimes I miss who or where we were in the past, but most times, I am proud of who we are and where we've come or where we can go. Even now. No matter how much time we have together.

·····

You have said we have done all we can do. That this is who we are and nothing can change that. But you and I have changed through the years. Separately and together. We will continue to change. Separately and together. Don't become a victim of who you think you are or are supposed to be. You are stronger than that. Always know you can become.

·····

I would do it all over again.

·····

Thank you for loving me. It doesn't matter that you loved me imperfectly or I loved you imperfectly. We are each imperfect, so why would we expect anything else? But I still and will always believe that we loved better than most.

…..

Unconditional love. Under any condition. You might not be ready to receive it, but I extend it nonetheless.

…..

I know your thinking sometimes pushes down your feelings. Both are important. Let them work together.

…..

I wrote one more note the following weekend. I would hold onto it until the divorce was finalized.

My ex got to leave the marriage his way, and I got to leave my way. I left the cast iron skillet because he liked his fried eggs a certain way, and seasoning a new pan isn't a quick or simple process. I left him the tea kettle because hot tea soothed him. I left him the crock pot we used most often, because he'd be familiar with it, and I thought crockpot meals would be a good option with his work schedule. And I left him the handwritten words that I could only pray would encourage him at some point and remind him of the love I had for him, the commitment I had made to him.

I left a list of a few things he might want to restock soon. A week earlier, I had made a list of essentials each of us might need and went to Target after a car appointment. He made a car appointment right after mine and walked up to me in Target as if shopping together for split-household supplies was completely normal. He seemed hurt when I told him it was too awkward to shop together.

I left the house because he pushed me out of his life but also because I cared for him enough to give what he was adamant he wanted—no matter how deeply it hurt me. And I left because I respect myself and others who watched from nearby.

STEPS

7

I took a huge step forward. I lived on my own. Of course, sadness came with that step. So did peace and freedom. I didn't find myself holding my breath as much, wondering what would hit next. I could cry when I was sad without hearing my ex scream from several rooms away, *Just STOP it!* I didn't have to endure glares when I listened to worship music or watched something he didn't like on TV. I didn't have to be blamed for strained relationships because I held him accountable for some of his choices and wouldn't keep his secrets from the people closest to us.

But separating from him was difficult. I still had hope that perhaps something would change, that he would decide to at least try to work things out even though it would be costly, that it was worth some honest conversations. I found myself in an odd juxtaposition of hope—the hope of what could be healed and the hope of having the strength to continue to move forward when it wasn't healed.

About ten days after my ex's announcement, I had taken off my wedding band. It was Valentine's Day. It might seem too quick to some, but the vehement declarations my ex made about leaving the marriage made the decision to take off my ring clear to me. I took it off with a sense of sadness and peace, not anger and disgust. Even if I was willing to work through the difficulties he was having and walk through the dark places with him, I couldn't do so without his honesty and humility.

Someone close to him told me he doubted my ex would ever be able to set aside his pride to take a step back toward his family, even if that's what he eventually came to want. I hoped that wasn't true because I had seen his humility and compassion through the years. But I began to realize those qualities weren't as deep and genuine as I had thought. There had been many masks over the years.

I'm not a stranger to masks. I've never been deeply inauthentic, but I had struggled with what to share with others in earlier phases of life. I went through a season when I was deceptive in the name of trying to protect people. I didn't want to trouble them. I could fix things. I downplayed struggles. But that bit me in the butt. It harmed my marriage. And at that point, I was ready to change some things. So, about halfway through the marriage, we went to counseling, admitted the faults we each brought into the relationship, apologized to each other, forgave each other, and grew.

The journey I went through then and in the years that followed was humbling but beautifully freeing. It was as if the shell of who I thought I was or who I needed to be came off, and I was unburdened. I began to step into the truth of who God created me to become. There weren't drastic changes; most of the changes were internal, but they made a huge difference. I set aside remnants of pride and control and stepped into truth and faith that seemed to go deeper and purer with each passing day. My relationships were healthier. My focus was clearer. My life was fuller.

Emotionally and spiritually, I was in a healthy place when my ex decided to leave the marriage. Looking back, because he was walking away from God and focusing on his own needs and desires, I wonder if my security in God and my commitment to serving others, including him, made him squirm a bit. Sometimes, when we surround ourselves with darkness, light is blinding and uncomfortable. When we focus on self, we see others in a distorted way.

We choose many things about who we want to be and how we see ourselves. We choose what personas to project. We find comfort zones by limiting what we share. The more we develop authenticity, the more we long for deeply honest relationships; the less we need to engage our filters, since our lives become increasingly transparent.

We can't share everything with everyone. We need to be appropriate, but we sometimes use the excuse of being appropriate to rationalize our deception. Sharing appropriately does not push away honesty. Deception is not appropriate. We can be honest even as we discern what different people need to know. No matter what pieces we share, we withhold some wisely, not deceptively. When we hold back because of defensiveness, we hold back for the wrong reason.

Even in those early days of our break up, I often thought about how thankful I was to be in a good place with God and to have deeply settled into a lifestyle of authenticity. My friends and family knew me well. It would have been hard to conceal anything in those early days. I didn't have the energy to hide anything or deceive anyone. I was simply surviving. As I began to move forward, I didn't know what fractured pieces God would bring into my future. But I knew I could not go back in time, in my faith, or in my marriage. This realization made me grieve but also gave me hope as I began to feel that God was tending my fractured life. I could trust Him to make me whole.

The day I took off my wedding band wasn't a step away from my marriage; it was a step into who God says I am, making that a priority over who the world or a man (or anyone) says I am. Technically, I was still married. But as I was reading Scripture in my isolated room, Romans 9:25 jumped off the page: *As He also says in Hosea: I will call Not My People, My People, and she who is Unloved, Beloved.*

She who is unloved is beloved. I knew the context of that Scripture wasn't meant for my specific situation, but knowing I am God's Beloved is a truth that spoke directly to me. I took off my wedding band with an assurance of my identity and my partnership with God.

I am worthy.

I later had "Beloved. Romans 9:25" tattooed on my wrist.

I have never been a "defined by a man" kind of person. God and only God defines me and gives me purpose. But I loved being married. It certainly wasn't easy at times, but the struggles were worth the effort. I grew a lot through them. God refined my faith through struggles. I experienced His grace and mercy in my marriage. I learned humility. I learned partnership and truth and honesty. I learned sacrifice. All the things God was revealing to me in other areas of my life went into action in my marriage.

And I had a good marriage. Sure, it ended in a crappy way, but I had felt unconditionally loved for many years. A counselor once told us we had a good marriage that we just wanted to make better. I agreed with that. We partnered well. We complemented each other well. We respected each other well.

Until we didn't.

When he pulled the rug out from under me, choosing to empathize with him was a struggle. It's hard to believe you were ever unconditionally loved by someone who one day says you're not. But even though I was no longer what my ex wanted—even though the person I felt closest to and looked forward to living out the rest of my life with rejected and belittled me—I knew I was enough. I am enough. Yes, I am still growing and changing. There is always room to learn and improve. There are always things to let go of and things to grasp onto. Living a life of purpose is dynamic. It has bumps, potholes, and ruts in it, but those are simply part of the road, not the road itself.

Shortly after I moved out of the house, I jotted, "Oh, how I loved him. He was a man who pursued God and wanted to glorify Him. He wasn't perfect, but he was pursuant."

Pretty much everything I thought I knew had been upended. As I began to move forward, I alternated between overwhelming peace and overwhelming anguish. I felt immeasurably hurt and betrayed. But through it all, I still wanted to love my ex well. Determining what that type of love looked like in action wasn't simple. Sometimes it was active, but many times it involved restraint. Loving well included letting go and moving on.

I wanted my ex to see that he was deeply loved without conditions, and the best way I knew to show that kind of love was to point to God's love with everything I did. Unconditional love is never unhealthy; however, how we act it out can be. I didn't try to run back to my ex to fix things. That wasn't a safe place to be. He was consistently clear about his rejection. He was clear about what he wanted, and he didn't want me in his life anymore. But that didn't take away my commitment to loving him well. It just changed the way I expressed it. It was no longer personal. I didn't have much contact with him, because it was destructive. For reasons I still don't understand, he could not express kindness to me. There were no remnants of respect. Maybe it was an all or nothing thing for him. But for my own well-being, because I still deeply cared and wanted the best for him, I had to step aside.

I could still respect him in the interactions I had with others who were wrestling with the whole situation. I could choose not to let bitterness take root. I could pray often and trust God. I could continue to get emotionally and spiritually healthy, because if I decided to step away from God or let all the turmoil cultivate seeds of doubt and indifference, it wouldn't be long before I ended up in a similar place, focused on myself. And other people in my life are too important to me. My family and friends do life with me, and I do life with them. Sometimes that life is beautiful, and other times, it is horrifically fractured. Whether I'm the one who needs help with fragments of my life, or I'm the one helping those I love pick up their pieces, investing in relationships are vital to us all.

In those early days of stepping forward, the truths I had come to know about God shone through the dense fog which surrounded me. I began to reclaim those truths within the context of what was going on around me. And I often jotted notes:

God's mercy allows me to lose my marriage and see He is enough.

I can do all things in Christ who gives me strength.

My strength, courage, and identity come from God, even now, perhaps especially now. The core of me has not changed. I am asking God to refine me, taking away the unnecessary and strengthening the essential.

8

I was sexually assaulted as a teen. In the moment, I remember feeling as if I couldn't breathe. Not as if I was being smothered, but as if breath would break the distance I was creating between me and reality. Breath would make it more real. Of course, I was breathing, but even as I remember those moments, I still catch myself holding my breath. I am not sure I took a deep, intentional breath for several hours. It could have even been the next day.

.....

I caught myself holding my breath again as my ex tore my world apart. But this assault was different. First, it wasn't sexual or even physical. It was emotional and spiritual. And that not only seemed more intrusive but deeper and harsher. Second, this time it was someone I loved. Someone I trusted. Someone I'd chosen to do life with for over two and a half decades. Someone I'd been vulnerable with and intimate with. Someone I'd had struggles with, but we had fought through them and become better, as individuals and as a couple.

This assault was personal. There was no distancing myself from it. The person I'd let get closest to me, who knew my strengths and weaknesses. The one who had forgiven and extended grace to me through the years and the one I'd forgiven and extended grace to through the years. But now he was shoving me away, cutting me out of his life. He was disregarding the effect of his words and actions on me and others close to him, disrespecting me with his deception.

The coldness chilled me through my bones. I would not take a deep breath the following day or even the day after that. Breathing took effort, and it was usually a forced, shallow, just-enough-to-survive breath.

Survival mode tests many things.

When my survival mode kicked in after my assault as a teen, it looked quite different. I dealt with it the best I could, which was to shove it aside and continue on. It's not as if I didn't think I had options. I had a supportive and loving family and network of friends who would've been helpful had I told them. But I don't think I had the energy to reach out. I moved on.

But moving on doesn't mean the trauma or issues connected to it are left behind without a trace. I survived, and I continued to live life. My assault didn't seem to impact my life much until what I'd buried began to poke me at the most inconvenient and unsettling times. So, my freshman year of college, I began to untwist what was knotted up inside of me and deal with it in the ways that I knew of. I felt healthier, I moved onward. Then it started to gnaw at me again several years later. I dealt with it again, the best I could at the time, and moved on. It was odd to me how it seemed to surface in different ways in different seasons of my life.

I had shared my assault with my ex when we were first dating because I didn't want anything hidden from him as we laid the foundation of our life together. I shared the best I could. I was still untwisting it all myself. He was compassionate but understandably uncomfortable. As the years passed, I realized he dealt with it much like I had. He buried it, then dealt with it when forced to over the years, when it started to interfere with his daily life, whether something at work triggered the memory, or he and I experienced something in our relationship that seemed to be impacted by it. I tried to help him and reassure him he could deal with it the way he needed, encouraging him to be patient with himself.

I tried not to take it personally when he ignored how something might impact me or refused to see how something I was struggling with might be connected to my own healing process. It was an odd balance for me at times, dealing with the waves of my own healing while trying to be patient as he dealt with the second-hand effects in his own way. It rarely came up, but when it did, I thought, "He's not really dealing with this. It's too much for him," usually followed by, "but doesn't he do this stuff for a living? How many people has he helped but can't apply his advice to himself?"

It's a challenge for all of us. Guiding others is sometimes a bit more comfortable than putting what we suggest into practice in our own lives.

When I was in my mid-30s, it all sort of boiled over for me, and of course, that impacted my marriage. My ex and I went to counseling and worked through some of our issues, with both of us bringing baggage to the relationship. The counselor confirmed we weren't in a horrible place but just needed to work on healing and growing together.

So we did the tough work together. I had work to do as an individual, too. In general, I made good decisions, but I had some faulty foundation work that needed to be reworked. When I was assaulted, I didn't have a good relationship with God. I didn't filter much through Him. I didn't trust Him with much, because I didn't know Him well. That had changed dramatically in the years that followed, but I hadn't revisited the trauma and healing process through His perspective and promises.

Revisiting and walking through it with God changed everything for me. It didn't make it all easy, but it gave me purpose and peace through it all.

Looking back, I realized my life would go on without much of a hitch until I'd hit some sort of pothole or speed bump, and I would suddenly find myself being pulled back into the same pain that I'd experienced as a teen. It happened every few years, and it didn't seem to be precipitated by anything in particular. It took shapes that didn't seem remotely related to the original pain. But it was.

In an instant, I would suddenly feel the intensity of that struggle from years before. I'd feel vulnerable and disregarded. God gave me the analogy of someone being badly burned. Of course, I've thankfully never experienced that specific pain, but I've had it described to me.

The first thing that's important to do is pull the person away from the fire. Separate the person from the source of the pain. Healing doesn't begin immediately. In fact, the burns continue. There are many things that cannot happen in those first moments and hours, things that can only be done as time passes. That original pain is horrific. And it is not the only time it will be felt.

Time must pass. No skin grafting or reconstruction can take place right away. I'm sure I'm not explaining this in a technically correct way, but the body has to rest and settle into recovering from the trauma. Only when the body begins to readjust can the next step take place.

Removing the burned skin is excruciating. It's a reminder of the pain of the burn. It's like stepping back into the pain. But it's different. It's a step in the healing process.

Then the skin must recover again. It swells because of the stress. Only as it adjusts can more procedures be performed. And there are often many procedures over time. Each time skin is grafted and reconstruction takes place, there is pain—pain that reminds the person of that original trauma.

That's how I felt. Every now and then, I felt pain that seemed to pull me back to that original trauma. In reality, while it was reminiscent of the same pain, it was pain that was part of the healing process. I felt as if it was pulling me back, but instead, God was prompting me forward. It's as if, with each season of struggle, there was a standing stone that marked a point of healing. I had a new perspective. I wasn't trudging back to that original pain any longer. I could look back and see a series of standing stones and know that God had been at each of those points in my life and every place in between. Yet I was continuing to move forward. God was healing me through the journey. Not only could I see how He'd guided me in the past, but I could glance into the future and expect that He would be with me and help me erect standing stones there as well. We would continue together.

I would be faithful in my "here," and God would lead and prepare me for my "there."

That realization was over fifteen years ago. While I knew God well before then, that season of my life felt like a turning point. So many wonderful things were birthed through that time, some which had been growing for years but began to bear fruit. Some things got pruned from my life; some things came into focus. The way I saw God changed. The way I saw myself changed. The way I saw pretty much everything in my life changed, because I had a renewed focus. I could see more clearly.

Of course, I've had struggles since then, but those struggles have been in a different context. Much of the junk that had been weighing me down was tossed aside, and some of it was used as solid building materials that turned some of my weaknesses into strengths. The insecurities that caused issues in my marriage were replaced with authenticity and accountability. None of the issues of mine that were primary reasons my ex and I went to counseling resurfaced again—well, at least not in reality. I think he, every now and then, began to fear there were problems that weren't actually there, and he would rationalize accusations that brought up old hurts. While it stung at times, I usually had peace about his fears and accusations, because I could stand on truth. I'd encourage him to explore the facts and tear something apart to find the truth, and every time, he'd discover what he imagined wasn't consistent with reality.

But sometimes people imagine what they expect to experience or want to experience for long enough that it becomes their version of reality. And that causes issues for the person as well as for everyone around him or her. Still, it doesn't change the truth.

9

I struggled to breathe as my ex betrayed and disrespected me, but I now had a different relationship and history with God. I knew Him. I trusted Him. And especially over the last dozen-plus years, I had yielded to and drawn near Him in a way that gave me a clear sense of security and peace in the midst of the worst mayhem of my life.

I wanted my ex in my life. I enjoyed partnering through life with him. We weren't perfect—no couple is—but we were good together. We'd raised two daughters together, and we'd worked through differences that go along with parenting. We'd adjusted to different jobs and responsibilities. We'd walked through some tough financial times early in our marriage. We'd gone through health issues. We'd taken amazing vacations together. We'd talked about retirement and becoming grandparents. We'd loved each other well.

But I couldn't make him stay. I could try to love him well through the process. I could try to encourage him instead of tearing him apart. I could offer options of counseling, separation, and honest conversations, but I couldn't make him choose any of those things. I couldn't make him tell me the truth of what was going on. I'm not sure if even he had all the pieces at the time.

But no matter how harshly he shoved me away, he couldn't shove me away from God. He didn't have that power. Even in those early hours and days, I remember the depth of my gratitude for my relationship with God, reflecting not only on the recent years but even the past months and weeks. The intimacy I'd had with God and the clarity of my perspective prepared and nourished me in ways I could have never foreseen.

Seeing coldness in the eyes of the man I wanted to live and die with perplexed and wounded me, but it didn't define me.

Within those first few days, my ex declared we could get a quick and simple divorce and save money by going through mediation. I didn't want a divorce at all, whether it was quick and simple or not. But I'd try it. I sat across from my ex during one of those meetings and saw the shell of the man I'd built a life with. He looked similar, but he didn't sound the same. He didn't respond the same. His harshness was cutting.

It's my opinion that no one wins in a divorce settlement. It's too costly for both people, as well as for the families involved. I live in a no-fault state and everything pretty much comes down to a mathematical formula. Sure, someone might get more or less of a piece of property or investment, but the bottom line ends up pretty much being 50/50. Each person loses half—not to mention the costs of the process, the emotional toll, the relationship death, and so on.

There I sat, in the same room as the person I had once known better than anyone else but was now an odd and unpredictable stranger to me. And I heard him declare that I might have to stay married to him because he wasn't sure he could afford to divorce me. Then he walked out.

I sat stunned for a moment. Could the person who was closest to me hurt me the worst? Did he feel that kind of hate toward me? Was it that easy for him to explode and walk out?

Of course, I knew he was just upset. He didn't want to stay married to me even if it cost him. We would both have costs that would dig deep into our pockets and, more importantly, our hearts.

Before anything else was said in that room, I took a breath of reassurance. My ex wasn't the person closest to me. God was. And while life with God certainly isn't easy at times, He wouldn't hurt me by rejecting me. He would never be hateful toward me. It's not who He is. It's not His character. I can trust Him, and that gives me certainty even in the chaos.

It's odd how clarity can be painful yet essential. There are about a half dozen moments of vivid clarity which happened between the moment my ex announced he was leaving the relationship and the date the divorce was final. That moment in mediation was one of them.

A couple people contacted me that evening to express concern for my ex, and for my own peace of mind, I drove by the house we had briefly shared. I saw him walking through the house he loved so much, the one we'd bought only months before, the house that would soon be his. I no longer was wanted there, nor belonged there. But at least I could sleep that night knowing I had checked on him and he was physically okay.

That night was one of few times I drove by the house. I had no reason to be on that side of town. But months later, something prompted me in that direction. I was driving home from a dinner with friends, and I listened to the lyrics of the song on the radio:

Tell your heart to beat again
Close your eyes and breathe it in
Let the shadows fall away
Step into the light of grace
Yesterday's a closing door
You don't live there anymore
Say goodbye to where you've been
And tell your heart to beat again
(Danny Gokey, *Tell Your Heart to Beat Again*)

I had already physically closed the door behind me, but there was something about driving up to the house that night, many months after I had moved. A peace washed through me. There were many more hard moments to come, but as far as moving on from the life I'd shared for a brief time in that house with the man I loved, that night set me free. I prayed for my ex and his new life. I drove away and sighed as I pulled into my small rental house. I was home.

10

Being fractured into wholeness is a process. There were times I felt surrounded by darkness, but the light within me was small and mighty, giving me hope and assurance. Other times, I felt as if I could spread my arms wide and relax my head back, ready to experience whatever God brought my way.

As time passed, I was able to catch a glimpse of God's perspective more often. In the Bible, when Joseph—the favored son with the coat of many colors, who was despised by his jealous brothers—faced his siblings after many years of separation, he declared, "What you intended for evil, God used for good." They had treated him horribly, throwing him into a pit and selling him to passersby. They let their pride and jealousy guide their decisions and lied to their dad about what had happened to Joseph. But Joseph survived. He lived through quite the ordeal, but he let God do the guiding and speaking. He let God reveal the truth—about God, about Joseph, about his brothers, and about the purpose of the many years that followed their decision to betray him.

I felt like Joseph as my ex shoved me out of his life. It was as if I was standing in a pit and looking up to see him towering over me with a cold disregard in his eyes. Even as he betrayed and deceived, God was reassuring me. Even as I was shoved into a pit, I knew God had my hand. He stood in the light, so no matter how dark it got, I had access to the light and truth. God wasn't towering over me with disregard. He sat on the side of that pit's edge and kept His hand on me the entire time. He reassured me with His presence and His promise to draw purpose through every single thing I experienced.

I felt as if my ex was trying to bury me. I felt and smelled the dirt kicked on top of me. But all the while, even as I struggled to breathe and even as I felt as if at any moment I was going to suffocate, something inside me told me to remember I am a seed and I would grow again, that I would fight for the light.

What he intended for evil, what he intended to destroy me, God would use for good. I don't understand the whole purpose yet. I know part of the purpose is to help others because God continues to give me strength and peace to share my story authentically.

When we're in a situation that seems unsettling and uncomfortable, we often want to avoid it. We might run away as fast as we can, or let things simmer until they either boil over or boil dry. But there are important lessons to learn during those unsettling, uncomfortable moments and seasons.

Like whitewater rafting, as much as we want to sit back and completely relax in those calm waters, there's a lot to be done between the rapids. We need to be intentional about healing, taking inventory, learning more skills and strengthening our muscles, planning ahead, and letting God recharge and prepare us for what is ahead.

While I was on my writing retreat just prior to the implosion of my marriage, I had written and scheduled many blog posts. I post daily, usually about a week or two ahead of time, but on my writing retreat, I was able to schedule over two months of daily posts. I had no idea what was coming when I wrote each one, yet God used those posts in the dark days that followed. I didn't have the energy to write, except for the few words at a time I could jot on my phone. People who knew what was going on often thought my blog posts were written in direct response to my struggles, but the posts were simply the sprouts of what God had planted earlier. He knew what I would need. He poured into me at the retreat, then He used some of that same nourishment I thought He had given me for others to remind me of His truth and goodness.

As a writer, I often look back on what I've written and wonder, "What was I thinking?" We all grow and change, but writers are dumb enough to document the whole process. Most of the time I look back on something I wrote, I am thankful for the growth, or I am simply reminded of a truth I need to claim yet again. But sometimes I chuckle at myself and what I was processing. And I hope I didn't take too many people down the rabbit trail with me.

But God is bigger than my distractions and tangents.

What I've learned in the light continues to permeate the darkness. Those dark moments and seasons are not times to make big decisions. That's something I said repeatedly to my ex as our marriage swirled in pieces around me. I had never known him to react that harshly and unwavering. Yes, he could be determined and stubborn. He could react rashly. But this was different. It was as if he took a machete to his life and cut a huge section of his history and many relationships tied to it and let it fall off the chopping block. As hurt as I was, I knew he was bleeding as well. Because of my love for and commitment to him, I knew I could help. I reminded him to take his time, but he was convinced he had thought through all the options and this was the only feasible one for him.

It's difficult to watch the people we love feel backed in a corner with limited options, even when they've positioned themselves there with their choices. When we stop doing life authentically with others, especially people who know us best, we can slip into rewriting reality. We make pieces of life much worse or better than they are. We look for new relationships so we can pick and choose what to share. The people in these new relationships will have a reality which matches ours. We avoid the people who will call us out on the inconsistencies, ask us tough questions, and hold up a mirror so we can glimpse ourselves in our distorted reality.

I felt bad at times, because I realized my ex must have stood at a series of crossroads. I don't know if he paused and struggled with which road to take, or if he forged ahead without realizing the options around him, but I imagine he must have felt alone at times. We all do.

But none of us are ever completely alone. I think sometimes aloneness becomes a self-fulfilling prophecy. We're uncomfortable with our own selves, so we pull back a bit, hesitant to share with others. Maybe we just don't know how or what to share with others. We've been hurt before, or we assume we know how someone will respond. We reach out and someone doesn't have time right at the moment and we give up trying again. We know what someone else is going through and don't want to burden him or her. Whether or not we have a valid reason, excuse, or rationalization, we begin to separate ourselves from others. We walk alongside them during our routines, but we don't truly do life with them.

We need people whether we acknowledge that need or not. And we don't just need them to affirm us. We need the discomfort that doing life with someone else brings. We need the humility and sacrifice. Support, encouragement, and accountability are not one-way streets.

Sometimes we don't even know how we're isolating ourselves. We can feel as if we are being ourselves in a variety of places and roles. For instance, we find a comfort zone because of the limitations of the workplace. We obviously don't share everything about our lives with our coworkers. We choose to share other things, including different parts of ourselves, with other groups of people, such as, friends, classmates, family, church, etc. It is not that we hide pieces of ourselves, but more that we bring out different pieces of ourselves.

Our true selves are the whole, not the one in which we are currently most comfortable or spend the most time. Discerning what to share with others makes sense. It's wise to have boundaries, but when we start to rationalize what we share and don't share because we're compartmentalizing for our own comfort and safety, we build a persona that isn't authentic. Some boundaries keep us healthy. Others spiral us into unhealthiness.

There were brief glimpses of my ex's vulnerability. He seemed to receive occasional moments of compassion from me well, but then a wall would suddenly go up. The coldness would return, and I began to realize, as much as I loved and cared for him, I couldn't make him receive what I could offer.

We can extend our hand but the other person doesn't have to receive our gift. Likewise, others extend their hands to us but we do not always accept their gifts. Watching my ex reject what I and many others were trying to offer him was difficult. It felt similar to being a parent and watching a child who wants to do something a certain way, convinced it's the best option even when the parent can see other options and many of the consequences ahead. Yet when a child is so intent, even in making a mistake, sometimes the parent knows the child has to learn the costs and the lessons on his or her own. It is hard to watch. But we can't force what we know on someone else just as they can't force what they know and prefer on us. As for my ex, I hoped that he would eventually work through the pieces of his life. I could continue to pray God would help him sort through the truth and self-deception.

We need to discern what we should and shouldn't receive from others, and that requires a firm trust in truth. When we're not in a healthy place in our lives, it's hard to know what to accept and what to reject. It's hard to know how to accept well and how to reject well. Our response matters.

Even though I wanted to fix what was right in front of me, I began to accept that I couldn't. But there was plenty I could do. Plenty I could give, and plenty I could receive.

God reminded me over and over of humility, and He enriched and strengthened me through it

.

11

It was difficult to get outside my own head and my own hurt at times, but pouring into others helped. When I caught myself consumed with my own stuff, I prayed for others. I texted people to check in and encourage them. I wrote notes. I volunteered. I engaged with people in the community and made new friends and served strangers. I became on high alert for people in need, and there was comfort in being able to pour into others.

I don't suggest pouring into others in an effort to ignore your own issues. Serving others can help us maintain humility. (It can also inflate our pride, so be aware of your motivation.) It can help us take the focus off ourselves long enough to appreciate the bigger picture. It multiplies joy.

Ministry is important to me. Not just formal ministry, a position in a church, but daily ministry—fulfilling God's purpose and reaching out to others to help, encourage, and teach. Several people asked me how I thought the divorce would impact ministry for me. How was I supposed to know? I didn't even know how the divorce would impact my daily life and relationships. But I knew one thing. Ministering from a healthy place is important to me. The goal is to help others. Our motivations, mindset, and baggage affects the impact we have on others.

There's a difference between ministering out of health and ministering out of perfection. Everything doesn't need to be going well in your life to help others. If you think you have to have all the pieces together in order to pour into others, you need to rethink your approach to ministry. You aren't perfect and never will be; you don't have all the pieces together.

But ministering out of your pain is tricky. Even with good intentions, we can end up harming others because of our own junk. Of course, God can reframe and repurpose what we offer, but I think we sometimes don't discern what we're offering to others for Him and what we're spilling onto others because we want to feel needed or process through our own stuff.

I spoke at a women's event several years ago, and the worship leader tried to weave some of her own story into the sets, as many will do. Only she overshared raw details. It was uncomfortable, as if we were sitting in her bedroom listening to her talk to herself in the mirror or reading her journal as she wrote in it. It felt intrusive.

On the way back to our accommodations, one of the hosts said, "I don't want to put anyone in an uncomfortable position, but I'm concerned about how the women might be feeling after the evening. Was it just me, or was that uncomfortable and inappropriate?" We all agreed we felt bad for the worship leader, wanting her to heal and grow beyond her struggles, but we also needed to acknowledge the wounds likely opened among people who listened to the rawness. We talked about how we could curb the effects without making things even worse for the worship leader. And we talked about the importance of discerning what to share with whom and when.

I wanted to be authentic as I went through the process of being fractured and devastated. I didn't want to hide from people. Well, there were times I *wanted* to hide, but I knew others would keep me in check. Because many knew my ex and me as mentors and leaders, and he disengaged swiftly, people were reeling, confused by it all.

When there are significant fractures in relationships, there is a small circle of immediate impact. But there are also a lot of ripple effects, especially the more connections that have been made through the years. Many friends immediately rushed in to check on me and try to help. They also reached out to my ex, but in most cases, he didn't respond or replied with hostility or disregard. When we're hurting, it's easy to claim, "It's none of your business," but we also claim people don't care if they don't reach out. Many people who would have never reached out to me did so in the weeks and months that followed simply because they couldn't get a response from my ex or received a response that baffled and concerned them. Had he not been so compassionate and generous to pour into many of them through the years prior and, in many cases, help them through marital issues, perhaps it wouldn't have seemed so odd. But it was unsettling to many.

After a few men who my ex had particularly helped through the years reached out to me to see if I could provide any insight or suggestions of how they could help him, I began to think of and pray for the people he'd helped over the years. I created a list of people I knew he had mentored or impacted in some way, and I asked a couple of his friends to share names if they were comfortable doing so, especially people who came to them with confusion or anger. The focus was to pray for each of them on a regular basis. When someone we respect and follow for years takes a very different path and leaves our lives, we're hurt, confused, and disoriented. We might question their character and the advice they gave us. I emphasized that if what he had advised them passed the truth test and was helpful and healthy at the time, they should probably still trust it.

We shouldn't throw out all the influence someone had in our lives just because he or she changes. We also can't simply follow the winds of change someone else is going through. We don't follow a person; we follow truth. We need to extend grace and patience to people. We're all growing and struggling and doubting. We need to discern what people teach us. We shouldn't assume everything is truth because we trust them or assume everything is wrong because we don't trust them. It all needs to be filtered.

But not all filters are trustworthy. We need to be aware of the filters we use. Ask yourself, "How do I determine what's true? What triggers make me doubt something? How do emotions and memories play into what and who I trust? Do I go to others more for affirmation or accountability? What might I need to change to know truth more deeply?"

It would be nice to trust that everyone around us applies common sense and common decency to their decisions, but neither is as common as we'd like. We need to be more intentional than assuming the best or the worst from people. We need to discern with wisdom what to apply and what to set aside. We can't just look for what affirms us and reject everything else. Although that would be the easy way, I'm glad God led me the hard way instead.

I knew better than to encourage people to blindly affirm me. I accepted encouragement, but I did not want it stripped of accountability. I wanted truth. I didn't want bitterness or bad-mouthing. I didn't get into lengthy conversations that focused on mulling over my ex's odd behavior. I didn't get into blame games. I encouraged people to reach out to him as they felt comfortable doing so. I didn't try to give all the answers of how people should or shouldn't respond. That was for them to decide. I didn't encourage people to believe they had to choose between the two of us. If they had a relationship with both of us, they should try to have a continued relationship with each of us if they wanted. There was no choosing sides.

Of course, people sometimes lean toward one person or the other when a couple splits. Sometimes it's the person they've known the longest or hung out with the most. It might be the person they have the most in common with, or it could be the person who makes an effort to stay engaged in his or her life. In general, people who said something along the lines of, "I love you both. I hurt for you both," did their best to stay engaged with each of us. They might now be closer to only one of us based on a variety of factors, but they treated us both with grace and respect and did not bad-mouth anyone.

People who said, "I don't want to get in the middle of it," usually took a different approach. It might look similar in the end—connected more to one than the other—but their tactic wasn't to engage each of us with respect but to avoid the situation as much as they could. They rationalized not asking any questions because they didn't want to have to choose. But there is a way to ask questions that shows more respect for people than to not ask questions at all. Avoidance is often received as disrespect or disinterest. If you don't ask, how does someone know you care?

Some people prefer avoidance, usually because they are uncomfortable with the topic or confrontation. But as uncomfortable as it is, when in the middle of crises, we need people to engage and ask questions. Care enough to ask questions. You don't have to grill someone and drive them away. Even when you are gentle, you might annoy someone. But avoiding annoyance isn't the goal when you want an authentic, growing relationship with someone. Going through the motions might make you or the other person comfortable for the time being, but it won't deepen your relationship.

One of the hardest early challenges for me was telling people close to my ex, whom he had refused to reach out to, about him leaving the marriage and the church. More than once, I heard the words coming out of my mouth that went through a basic summary of, "Here's what happened, and I really can't give you more details, because I don't really understand it all myself." And I saw people's faces—his friends, people who loved him. They were pained, and I felt horrible about causing that pain. And I was angry that I was in a situation in which I was telling his friends because he wouldn't have contact with them.

As much as that frustrated me, I tried to step beyond my own feelings in those moments. They loved him, and for that, I loved them, too. I knew they were hurt, and if I could help them through that hurt, I would try to be as patient and honest as possible.

The conversations got a bit easier over time. Perhaps it was because once the people closest to us both knew, the next wave of people were acquaintances, who had no idea anything had happened. They usually simply said something like, "I haven't seen him around for a while. How is he? Everything okay?"

I gave short answers that were to the point. Usually, "He decided he didn't want to be married any longer." The hurt, tears, and confusion on people's faces still saddens me.

When I gave a similar response to one person who asked about him, she looked confused and said, "Oh, I'm sorry. I thought you were (my ex's name)'s wife. I must have mistaken you for someone else."

No, I am who you think I am.

"But he would never do that."

I gave her a hug as she began to cry and say, "I'm so sorry" over and over.

People needed reassurance. They needed the truth. They needed to try to understand. They needed to see that I was going to be okay.

And, although I knew that I would be okay, I struggled immensely. I hurt deeply. I cried often and sometimes found myself on the floor of my house, paralyzed by grief and hurt. People needed to know both those truths: I would be okay, and I was devastated. Sharing anything less would be incomplete.

God never let me stay in the dark places for long. I needed to be on the floor sometimes, in the depth of the horribleness of it all. But it's not where I lived. I resided in the reality of it all, which included filth and betrayal and truth and hope. It was a horrible place to be, and it was a beautiful place to be.

Light pierces the darkness, but the darkness is still there.

Hope is stronger than despair.

It just doesn't feel that way sometimes.

THE CHURCH

12

Some people find judgement in church, but that wasn't true for me. I found peace and grounding.

I was on staff at the church at the time. That first staff meeting was difficult. I needed to be at work. I needed a sense of normalcy. But nothing was normal. My world was spinning. I looked horrible and felt horrible, but I didn't want to hide.

I could hardly get the words out to tell my friends in that meeting room. Once again, the hurt on their faces crushed me. I knew the hurt was for themselves, who loved both my ex and me, as well as for me and for him. They gathered around me and prayed, and I sobbed. It was a beautifully sad but hopeful moment.

That small group of people were amazingly respectful in the weeks and months to come. It became evident to me that they loved me well, not because of who I am but because of their faith in God. They were gentle with me at times but didn't shove anything under the rug. They asked questions that needed to be asked but didn't gossip. It still amazes me how many people had no idea what had happened months later, because these friends and colleagues respected me and the marriage enough to be patient with the process.

It wasn't just that group of people but so many others in church as well. Just a few weeks into the mayhem, I saw one of my ex's good friends and his wife. They were so special to both of us, but he was particularly close to them. They didn't know anything yet, and I didn't want them to find out from someone else, so I asked them to step into the office with me. Would I ever get used to the pain on people's faces? It was as if I could see their hearts tear in front of me. I held it together and gave them hugs, but I fell apart once I left that room. I walked through a crowd of people to get to a hallway to escape.

Halfway down the hallway, I felt a hand on my shoulder. I swung around and saw a woman who looked me in the eyes and declared, "Susan, there are people who love you here. You are hurting. Don't run from them. Let them love you."

She was right.

Church is often known as a place littered with hypocrisy and judgement. We foster those stereotypes with our inauthenticity. We imagine what others will say or think, and we avoid being with them because of what we're imagining. But I was a proponent of authenticity. I spoke and wrote on the topic often because of my own struggles. And I wasn't going to run away.

I nodded at the woman, grabbed some tissues, gave her a hug, and walked back toward the crowd. (I found out how important it is to have tissues strategically and generously placed throughout the church building. It was almost as if our custodian could foresee exactly where people would need them, because anytime I needed a tissue, a box seemed to be within reach.)

I didn't notice anyone looking at me oddly. Maybe it's because I didn't have the energy to consider those innuendoes. What I noticed were the people willing to make eye contact, walk by and say, "I love you and I'm praying," or simply give me a quick hug or squeeze on my shoulder. It was the smallest expressions of love that fed me well.

And I was sad that my ex could not experience and accept the same kind of support.

Sometimes we don't experience compassion or reconciliation because neither is extended to us. But many times, I believe we don't experience compassion or reconciliation because we're not open to accepting it. Our expectations get in the way. We declare all sorts of things, like people are being nosy or judging us or gossiping. We assume their intentions, which makes it easier for us to reject their efforts to reach out to us. In the process, we might protect ourselves from a few ill-intentions, but we miss out on many good intentions.

When we get caught up in our own perspective and pride, when we only want to see things through the lens of what we need and want, we play a wild game of pinball. Maybe a lot of people don't know much about pinball anymore, but it was a pretty cool arcade game. Pull back the knob and let it fly, sending a ball onto the slanted floor of the game. Then use the side buttons to strategically move levers to hit the balls and fight the gravity forcing them to the bottom to end the game.

There is strategy to the game, but many people think if they just keep hitting the side buttons over and over, chances are good they'll hit the balls and delay the end of the game. They do this instead of really watching what's happening and choosing the best moments to hit those buttons.

The more baggage we have with church and with people in general, the more wildly we punch those side buttons. We think if we keep moving and stay defensive, surely we'll ward off ill-intentions. And we probably will to some degree, but we'll also spend a lot of defensive energy and miss out on some of the best connections of our lives.

Church people—any people—are not perfect. Someone will gossip, but that doesn't mean everyone gossips. Someone will not talk to you, but that doesn't mean no one will talk to you. Someone will judge you unfairly, but that doesn't mean everyone will. Someone will inaccurately apply the teachings of Scripture, but that doesn't mean everyone will. All those mistakes—whether they're intended or not—happen outside the church, too. It's a people thing not a church thing.

The church has gotten a lot of things wrong through the centuries. But it's gotten some things right, too. We learn as we go, and some of that learning seems to have to happen again with each generation. Even each of us as individuals seems to have to go through our own lessons instead of picking up where those before us left off.

I do believe the church must be held to a higher standard. People in the church should be among the first to forgive, to reach out to people in need, to be generous, to be patient and loving. And we're not. But we also are. We're trying. Or at least some of us are. We're trying to grow, and that process takes a lot of humility and effort and time.

I'm sorry if you've been hurt by the church.

Please don't shut out God because you despise or are uncomfortable with the church. Seek truth. Wrestle through faith with bold honesty. Ask questions and express your doubts. Do it with others—inside or outside the church—who agree and disagree with you. Sharpening one another takes effort, kindness, patience, and a ton of grace.

It's worth the effort.

13

I hope my transparency about what was going on in my life stirs some conversations in the church: How do we deal with divorce? More than that, how do we deal with a myriad of challenges? How do we deal with the things that fracture people's lives? How do we deal with the issues that tear apart relationships?

None of those questions have easy answers. If they did, I'm pretty sure someone would have figured it out and packaged it by now. But relationships and individual growth are not programmable or predictable.

The relationships we build and the conversations we have matter. We need to get to know each other. We need to notice people and invest in them. We need to let them into our lives, too. It's risky, and it takes time. Conversations can be ongoing and casual, and they can also be difficult and uncomfortable. It's easy to just pass by each other instead of sitting face to face. We can easily get into a habit of playing a game of tag, where we only make quick connections with the people familiar to us. Perhaps we prefer dodgeball, as we avoid the people we don't like.

As time passed, I found myself in a multitude of conversations about why we aren't better at talking about things in church. Why do we feel we have to hide things? Why are we hesitant to approach someone and ask questions that might be uncomfortable?

I've wondered some of these same things, but more conversations are going on than we might know. We assume no one is saying the tough stuff to someone who needs to hear it. But often, either that person is rejecting what's being said, or people are reaching out in private. That's not to say we should assume someone else is doing the hard stuff, or that we are off the hook. If we think someone should be reaching out, maybe we're that someone.

We need to keep in touch with people, so that we know them well and notice the signs of inconsistencies in their lives. If we distance ourselves and have superficial contact, we don't know enough to be helpful to one another. Still, we have to realize we can't know everything. And because we can't know everything, there's another relationship that has to always take precedence: it's the one we have with God.

One of the very best things you can do for the people around you is consistently strive to be spiritually healthy. When you are, other sorts of health will follow. On the other hand, when you are spiritually unhealthy, health in other areas tends to deteriorate, including emotional and relational health. Church involvement does not predict spiritual health. I know plenty of people involved in church who are not spiritually healthy. Of course, we're all in process, but too many people don't care or notice that they've hit a plateau and refuse to grow and change.

Becoming spiritually healthy is a continual process. There's no one-time goal you can reach and camp under. There's no star sticker trophy you earn, then stop. When my ex announced he wanted a divorce, I was in a spiritually healthy place, and I knew it was important to stay on that track. Every decision I made was somehow grounded in that desire to stay healthy. I was sensitive to avoid what would make me feel good temporarily but could hinder continued growth. I had to pursue what was best and right and true. Making those decisions was not easy sometimes. I chose poorly at times, especially with my attitude. Those inner choices might not be visible to others, but they determine what spills out later. I'd seen that from my ex.

I knew people were looking to me as an example, for reassurance and understanding. That didn't put extra pressure on me. It would have at other times in my life, but when I committed to living authentically years ago, the pressure to appear to be a certain person dissipated. I was going to become the person God wanted me to be, and I knew that was a long process. I needed to stay focused on Him, and I knew that as I did, He'd use me in many ways I might never understand.

I still struggled with many things, but I didn't struggle much with what others thought. Would there be a stigma of being divorced? Maybe, but marital status didn't define me. It changed many things in my life, but it didn't change my value or influence. It shifted a lot in my life, but it didn't negate or diminish me.

I know many people are not in a good place when chaos hits their lives. Turmoil complicates issues already in place before the chaos happens. As we help others through crises, it's important to remember that we can't fix everything for them. We can't even give them the exact tools they need, because we don't know all the fractured pieces. We won't have all the answers, but we can be present. We can encourage them to focus, to breathe, and to take it one step at a time.

I had to remind myself to breathe sometimes. It seemed ridiculous, because, of course, I was already breathing. But I often caught myself taking shallow breaths or holding my breath for a few seconds. Friends reminded me to breathe. I bought a shirt with "Breathe" across the front. I frequently wore a necklace with "Just Breathe" stamped into it. I often reached up to rub my fingers on it as I controlled my breathing.

Breathing helped me slow down. It helped me seek truth. Because many of my friends share my faith, I often hear us say to each other, "seek God." I frequently modify that encouragement slightly to say, "seek truth," because I don't always know a person's relationship with God at a particular moment. Especially in crisis, our attitudes about God can surprise even us.

Even if we generally trust God, we tend to pick and choose the characteristics of God we want to focus on in any given situation. We compartmentalize and apply only what we want instead of what is best and true. Are we angry? Then let's seek God's justice. Are we sad? Let's seek God's compassion. Are we wracked with shame and guilt? God's forgiveness. Do we think someone else should feel shame and guilt? We turn to God's wrath. Just as we pull Scripture verses out of context to emphasize what we most want to believe and apply at a particular time, we pull out God's character traits based on what will benefit us the most at a particular time.

But that's not how God works. It's not who He is. His character encompasses all of his traits at the same time. I don't know how some of them coincide sometimes, but they do. That's God. Mercy and forgiveness reside with justice. Patience with perseverance. Compassion with accountability.

When we seek truth, because God is truth, we're also seeking God. But seeking truth can help narrow our focus. When we seek truth, we get to the basics. It's as if we simmer what's going on long enough for the nonessentials to evaporate. We don't seek truth to throw it in someone's face or prove someone wrong but to know what we can stand on. Getting to the truth of something helps us clarify our next steps. Truth doesn't make next steps easy, but it does make them more visible.

Many of us prefer our comfort over truth. And much of our encouragement to others perpetuates this mistake.

- Do what's best for you.
- You'll figure it out.
- You deserve to be happy.

Every single one of these options needs a truth check.

- Find truth, and whatever that involves will be best for you.
- Find truth, and you'll find your next steps.
- Find truth, and what follows will be much more important than happiness.

We have to be braver than simply making people feel better in situations. Yet we can't bash them over the head with truth either. We can certainly bring it up to them. We can help them as they seek truth. But unless they find and accept it, they'll likely not apply it.

In the church, we get into the habit of giving easy answers. Maybe it's not a church thing. We probably all have our standard easy go-to answers—most likely things that have worked for us—and it's easy to just pass the advice along to others. But the search for answers is a critical part of the answer itself. That's where relationships and authentic conversations come in.

When we're willing to journey together, we get to know people's struggles and doubts. We know their temptations, strengths, weaknesses, and gifts. We know what humbles them and what puffs up their pride. Because of those relational seeds we have planted and cultivated along the process, we have better insight as to how to handle a crisis when they face it.

We also need to realize people only share what they want to share. If they're intent on creating their own version of reality, and that's the only reality you have available, you might have a skewed view of where they are and how you can help. This is why authentic relationships developed with intentionality and over time are critical.

For example, my ex was raised in an "appearances matter" atmosphere: what others thought was important even if it meant wearing a mask and a fake smile. Some things were simply done out of obligation because they were expected. So when he began to have doubts about some core beliefs in his life, he masterfully hid the struggle from people. He went through the motions of serving, encouraging, and discussing. All the while, though, he was building a tangent life to satisfy needs he could not—or would not—share or acknowledge. The discrepancies eventually became more than he could bear, and deception and selective disclosure impacted many areas of his life.

That's what masks do when worn for too long. Many people around us are wearing masks. So do we, but we get used to our own. The more deeply we do life well with others, the more we get to know others' masks and the more willing we are to take ours off. Until we get to that place in the process, we won't speak into each other's' lives as clearly and effectively as needed in order to help each other handle the times of chaos effectively.

14

There's an older man at church who is usually quiet but always seems to be up to something. He has an ornery grin on his face much of the time. He's also one of the most generous servants, always willing to chip in and help. He's a man of few words, but I've always enjoyed our brief exchanges.

I was a bit surprised when he approached me several weeks into the ordeal. He looked me in the eyes and firmly said, "Don't give up. Keep going. If you get into trouble of any kind, call me. Maybe I can help." I was touched, and I think I made some sort of a sassy remark about finding it ironic that one of the biggest trouble makers I knew was offering to get me out of trouble. He smiled, then continued, "We need help from others. That's how this works. A wrench has to fit and come in contact with another tool or piece of something in order to be helpful. We were made to work together and help each other."

Oh, how right he was.

Friends and acquaintances reached out in so many ways.

People brought meals. They stopped by to check on me. They offered to help with yardwork. Even though I turned many offers away, either because I just needed some space or because I actually enjoy yardwork and other tasks, I appreciated every effort.

I came home sometimes to find a card or flowers or food. The first week in my new place, I received a gift card from a local restaurant and some flowers. I went to the china cabinet to choose a vase and selected one of my favorites.

It was the same vase I'd put roses for my ex in just a couple weeks before. When we were dating, I bought him yellow and red roses to let him know how much I treasured our friendship and our romance. He told me many times how deeply that gesture impacted him. So, a couple weeks after he said he wanted out of the marriage, and I found out the truth about another woman and other factors, I bought him yellow and red roses and placed them in his favorite room in the house. As hurt as I was, I wanted him to know that I cared. I suspected he would not receive my confrontation well when I asked him about his girlfriend, so I wanted to plant the seed of "I committed to you and love you no matter what."

While he seemed confused about the flowers, he kept them until I confronted him a couple days later about his girlfriend. Then he threw them away.

I tried.

I took the vase with me when I moved, and my first bouquet of flowers went into the same vase. It was an odd comfort to me. It reminded me that his rejection, his tossing aside of my gift and our relationship didn't mean all beauty or all gifts were gone. I still appreciated people in my life and the beauty they brought to it.

I was amazed by people's thoughtfulness. Whether they knew the details or not, understood or not, I received a lot of compassion.

I don't know what everyone's motives were. I suppose I could have seen some of their actions as intrusive or nosy. But regardless of others' intentions, I received most everything as thoughtfulness. I think the filters we use as we give and receive matter. Blaming filters? Comfort filters? Truth filters? The filters we use as we give and receive reveal what we most look for and expect. Perhaps I simply didn't have the energy to be on guard, or perhaps God reframed many interactions for me, but I was thankful.

I so wanted my ex to be able to experience some of the same compassion I was experiencing. I didn't want him to shut so many people out of his life—people who had been friends for years, who loved him and cared for him.

Sometimes our fear of judgement gets in the way of receiving people's love and compassion. Yes, that love and compassion might also involve some hard questions and truth checks, but would we expect anything less from the people we've done life with so deeply for years?

One of my friends texted me and asked, "I work hard on my marriage, and I think you did, too. Did you see a warning sign? Could this happen to me even if I'm doing everything I can?"

Yes, of course, it can. I don't say that to spur fear in anyone. Early in our marriage, my ex and I talked about how we didn't want to be a couple who said divorce would never be an option for us, because we believed that if we thought it could never happen to us, we'd let down our guard and be more susceptible. It kept us on our toes a bit more.

Until it didn't.

Sometimes we see signs but don't know what they mean at the time. Maybe we don't even realize they are signs. In an everyday context, they seem "everyday." Sometimes even the abnormal seems normal, because people get good at going through the motions and deceiving themselves and others.

There is always a possibility that one person will decide the marriage is no longer a priority, that getting out and starting something new is preferable. (There is also always a possibility someone who is on the edge of jumping ship in their marriage will decide to turn and do the hard work to stay.) We can pour into a relationship and believe we're doing everything we can yet still find out the other person has separated from us. Just like we can drive carefully but get in an accident or try to take care of our bodies but still get cancer. We have responsibility, but we don't have complete control.

Some people compartmentalize, and when crisis hits, compartmentalizing might help as a crisis coping mechanism. Temporarily. Compartmentalizing over time usually becomes harmful. In the immediate crisis, it allows you to get a few things done that are pressing but difficult to focus on. Over time, however, it creates silos which separate truths and reality. It is almost always accompanied by rationalization and excuses. In the process, all sorts of blame gets displaced, and a skewed perspective that makes sense in one compartment invites deception in other compartments.

Truth is always better than the comfort of compartmentalizing.

I think compartmentalizing has almost become a mis-valued skill in our culture. I've heard many declare, "I compartmentalize well" as a badge of accomplishment. But just because someone assigns value to a skill doesn't make it helpful or healthy.

Compartmentalizing will help you be content in one area, while closing off other areas of your life. Compartmentalizing as an ongoing strategy instead of a temporary crisis mode tends to split most everything into two categories. First, the areas of life people feel are going well, the ones they deem as healthy, are often attributed to their own efforts. Second, the areas that are not going well are often blamed on others. They deem responsibility over some areas, the ones they're proud of, but claim no control or influence in the areas they don't understand.

Compartmentalizing is often rationalized as an energy-saver. However, when the walls between the categories are torn down, we realize some insights and efforts help more than one category at once. When we look for truth and let that truth change us, we heal and grow in multiple areas. We become more whole.

Truth isn't always the easy way, but it is the most beneficial way to live fully and purposefully. Truth and wholeness walk hand in hand.

15

The process of being fractured into wholeness included a lot of friends and family and a lot of writing. My mom sent me a card nearly every week until the divorce was finalized eighteen months later (and several more cards afterward). Others sent cards and texts. I received comments on my blogs and social media posts. Many times, those notes—sometimes from strangers—were just what I needed at the moment. People provided encouragement for me to take one more step, share authentically, and heal at times I wanted to give up.

Perhaps a note or two from my friends will help you as well or will spur you to reach out to someone today. Send a note or a text. Meet someone for coffee. Speak truth into someone's life. It might just be exactly what he or she needs to hear to take the next step forward.

.....

Just wanted to take a minute to thank you for a little journal you gave me a few years ago...Probably in a Bible study. Something so small. But it's such a huge gift to me right now. I recorded some very precious prayers in there...I have never been a big journal person, So I almost never purchase them! But I am so thankful for the one you gave me! Thank you for investing in people in all of the big and the small ways! You make a difference.

.....

Just read today's blog *Hanging On For Dear Life*...exactly what I needed to read today, in fact I will probably read it repeatedly between now and Monday...when we find out if this treatment is working. Anyway just wanted to encourage you to keep writing, because you make a difference. Love you!

.....

You will be more than okay, but it will take time and much prayer.

.....

It's what we all desire: to be able to forgive and become the person God intended us to be despite our circumstances.

.....

I wish I could carry some of your pain for you, but only Christ can do that. Hold on tight. Satan is doing a number on you.

.....

Sometimes you might need to just scream and let junk out. Remember, God gave you that scream. That can be healthy.

.....

Praying for you all, and not the little prayers but mountain-moving prayers.

.....

I hate these times when you feel overwhelmed. These are the moments I wish I had more to give you than prayer and love alone. You are wise in setting boundaries and remaining in them even when you're tempted to step over. My heart breaks. If only he could see how far-reaching his choices are.

.....

I just put a card in your mailbox and left you a warm drink on your step.

.....

I am always in awe of what I read. Thanks for letting God permeate the pores of your pain.

.....

This world can suck, but God is always good. Praying for you as this journey continues, and praising all you are teaching us through your authentic openness.

.....

Thank you for sharing your journey. I am amazed by your perseverance and faith following such a deep hurt. Your story has made me stop and examine what I need to be doing in my own life.

Then there were texts I wrote in replies, moments I claimed truth and shared vulnerabilities. They continue to remind me where I've been and have hope for where I'm growing.

.....

Hope is firmly planted and will grow.

.....

I am just sad. Just grieving the man I have loved for so long. Or at least, the version of him I did life with for so long.

.....

Faith consumes and neutralizes fear. It is still there but God handles it much better than I.

.....

I am thankful for the blessings I can see among the rubble.

.....

I am stronger. It is not my own strength but I am glad God shares His. I feel He is preparing me for the future, and I see light piercing the darkness around me. I am ready to start serving others and look beyond my own little world and circumstances. I don't want to miss out on what God has purposed for me. I would rather His purpose involve the man I loved, but I will grieve and heal in time.

.....

Forgiveness doesn't change the need for safety and health, for boundaries and guidelines, but it loosens the binding on my heart. It gives me freedom and peace. The ability to not return to a situation of hurt but to move forward into healing. A vulnerability not to the person who betrayed and belittled me but to God who will prune me, mold me, comfort me, and challenge me.

.....

It's been a rough couple days, but I will be okay. I had a pity party on the couch for a couple hours, then made myself get up and go outside.

.....

God blesses me abundantly. I choose to seek and acknowledge Him, even in the hard times.

.....

I think sometimes God blesses me with vulnerability and weakness so I am better prepared to accept and rely on His strength. He is good. I am so grateful for Him.

.....

Oddly, I think my love has deepened because I now know I love my soon-to-be-ex unconditionally.

.....

This is just so stupid.

.....

Sometimes the smallest things become big when I see them through His eyes.

.....

I just want this to all be over. It hurts so much. I feel tossed aside and discarded even though I know that's not what God thinks of me.

.....

I am trying to focus on God and His blessings and setting aside the distractions of everything else. God gets all the glory of whatever He has purposed for me no matter how challenging it feels to me.

.....

Today I am simply thankful for who He is and how He continually pours into me. He overwhelms me.

16

Church became a reset place for me immediately. It wasn't always easy to face and interact with people, but it was good nonetheless. It was an intentional engagement with people who loved me and kept me in check. It was also an important part of my schedule, my routine. There were a lot of motions I couldn't go through, but Sunday mornings and other church events scattered through the week helped me maintain a semblance of sanity.

It wasn't the people as much as it was being with God among people. Worship became a sweet time. It was deeply healing to me. The act of surrendering, pouring myself out and letting God pour into me, overwhelmed me most Sundays. It was months before I made it through a worship service without crying. I was glad it was winter. It was scarf season. It had been a year earlier when my dad died, and I had learned scarves can come in handy for catching tears as they roll off my cheeks.

Worship is not just a routine for me. It's not a feeling. It's an intentional engagement with God. It's a surrender. And I sometimes catch myself pulling back, staying in my own thoughts and just going through the motions. Years ago, I caught myself singing without thinking about the words. It threw me off balance. So, I started to only sing the words as I considered and claimed them. If I caught myself going through the motions, I'd stop singing until I was engaged and ready again. During prayer, to avoid just listening instead of engaging, I'd quietly repeat everything the person praying was saying.

Worship is about life for me. It's how I choose to focus on God and live out His purpose on a daily basis. It creates the foundation of my choices, thoughts, and attitudes. It guides my relationships. Worship doesn't make me perfect; it makes me authentic. It positions me so I'm prepared to respond based on His prompts instead of my preferences.

There have been times I absolutely knew I was supposed to stop and help someone along the side of the road, and there have been many times I didn't feel that pull at all and drove by. There have been times I have listened and processed with people, yet other times I needed to walk away in the moment. There are things I write about at one point that seem awkward at another point and still other things I might not ever approach in my writing.

We get into so many scuffles about "if we're the hands and feet of Jesus and we're loving God and loving others, should we...[do this or that]?" We spend time arguing with people over our own convictions when God is working on them and their convictions with a different approach. Let's always leave enough space for Him to prompt people. Let's quit shaming people into what "if you're a true Christian" looks like.

I've looked like a pitiful Christian at times in my life, but that doesn't lessen my journey. Thankfully, God worked on me through every season and continues to do so. I'm thankful for His patience and perseverance. He's a lot more faithful than I am. But since He made me in His image, I have hope I'll continue to grow.

I can totally relate to the father in Mark 9:24 who says to Jesus, "I do believe! Help my unbelief."

One of my very favorite worship experiences was in North Carolina. I was a guest for the weekend at a women's event, and I went to Sunday morning services with the hosts. This was while my ex and I were still together and he had traveled with me since one of his best friends lived nearby. They would go to the friend's church, and I would meet them for lunch before heading to the airport.

Only I didn't make it to lunch, and I barely made it to the airport. I turned off my phone and didn't realize how close I would be cutting the time until I turned my phone back on and had many missed calls. Apparently, a four-hour service can feel like not much more than an hour and a half!

It's not so much that the time has to fly by, but I find that I fade when I surrender in a worship service. It's as if I become transparent, yet so many of my senses are heightened.

In those weeks and months that immediately followed my ex's split, I savored every moment of worship services. The songs seemed richer and deeper. The messages seemed more applicable. The air seemed fuller yet lighter. Worship was freeing and cleansing.

It was odd at first, because I was used to seeing my ex on the stage. He told me he wanted out of the marriage on a Friday night, and as usual, he was committed to serve on the worship team that Sunday. I couldn't muster the strength to sit in church and see him on stage when I knew he was about to leave family and friends. I stayed home. Only the few people I had told knew anything. People who saw him that morning said he joked and interacted as if nothing was happening. Then he left the church.

In the weeks and months that followed, I felt sad not seeing him there, but I knew his absence on the stage was just a sign of a deeper absence. The depth of his absence almost clarified the depth of God's presence for me. Clarity can be painful yet incredibly helpful.

Part of what was clarifying to me was the process of redemption. I was learning that redemption doesn't always look like what we expect.

There were several times I felt something so strongly and clearly during Sunday morning worship that it seemed almost real. Each time caught me off guard. In the middle of pure worship with thoughts focused completely on God, I sensed something happening that was not actually happening. I sensed—imagined—felt my ex walking into the room and cautiously slipping into the space beside me.

No words are said. I simply reach for his hand. He accepts. It is one step. A huge one. And there is a sense of peace.

Redemption.

I don't believe God is going to redeem the relationship in that way. Not that I don't believe He can; I just don't think that's the focus. God consistently reminds me of His pursuit of my ex. Despite his rejection of me, I know his rejection of God runs more deeply. I also know I can trust God. God pursues and redeems. Redemption is not always an exact rebuilding of what was destroyed. It is the rebuilding of people—our hearts and souls—not of situations and things.

And sometimes the redemption involves witness. There were several times someone would comment on how seeing me worship through pain helped them. It always caught me off guard. I didn't think about being a witness to anyone during Sunday morning services. I never felt as if anyone was watching me. I don't think it was ever invasive or nosy. At least it never felt that way to me. It was simply community worship.

A young family started coming to church, and while I didn't know them well, we had many common friends. One of those friends passed along to me something the mom said: "If Susan can worship like that with all she has happening in her life, I can worship often, too."

I wasn't doing anything special, and I don't pass that along to get any kudos. I didn't even know anyone noticed. But it was a reminder to me that people are often watching—again, not in a creepy, nosy way. But people notice other people. And the more authentically you live, what people notice accurately reflects you. We're not consistent all of the time, but the more authentic we are, the more consistent we are.

I have become more sensitive during worship in several ways. Sometimes the sensitivity is between me and God as we work through things. Sometimes the sensitivity is between me and others. Even if I don't say a word to someone, if I glance around the room and some people seem to stand out to me, I pray for them, trusting God knows what's going on with them right then and what they might need. Sometimes the sensitivity is to just be among people in God's presence. It's a sweet place to be.

I don't worship because I feel good but because God *is* good.

Worship reminds me of God's love. I wanted to love my ex and receive his love fiercely. It was an intense feeling, the desire to love him well no matter what but knowing he did not love me in return, which meant I needed to be careful. God set the boundaries to keep my tender heart protected. Worship constantly reminded me to yield to Him in all things. God knew how I felt. He knew my weak spots. I consistently asked Him to help me heal well and set the best boundaries. He consistently reminded me that He loves people and often doesn't get their love in return.

The difference is God doesn't want to be loved for His own sake as much as for the other person's benefit. And knowing that made choosing to love Him through the pain that much richer.

GRATITUDE

17

There were days when sadness clung to me like pesky plastic wrap. I couldn't shake it. I don't think we need to be happy in order to honor God. He gets our sadness. He grieves with us. But He also doesn't want it to consume us. He wants us to move through sadness, grief, and other emotions that can consume us and make us feel stuck. Each time we break free does not mean we are free from that particular experience forever. Most times, it is a process, just as I mentioned the healing process of someone who has been burned.

I often asked God to determine and become my posture, which meant I wanted Him to determine what was best for each moment. Sometimes I needed those flat-on-the-floor devastating moments. Other times, I needed to stand straight and tall. I needed times of rest, times of turning away, times of listening well and looking someone in the eyes. I needed to serve sacrificially and accept generosity. Whatever I was going through was being yielded to and purposed by God.

That doesn't make what I was going through easy.

My daughters and I had a trip planned about a month after everything exploded. We were going out of town to see a much-anticipated musical, spend the night, and meander around the city. It's something I normally would have deeply enjoyed. But this trip had been my ex's Christmas gift to us. His last Christmas gift to us, his last gift ever to me. And while I appreciate the memories I made with the girls that weekend, it was hard. I tried to stay focused on them and have a good attitude, but there were many times I wanted to stop and throw up on the sidewalk because the gift of the trip was tainted. I had trouble separating the joy of the trip with the truth I knew about my ex's choice to leave the marriage months earlier, building a relationship with someone else, and connecting with her throughout our family Christmas celebration. It made me sick.

But God strengthened me. He reassured me the feeling of sickness was okay to experience, the tears were okay to let fall, and the joy of being with the girls through a tough part of the healing process was a blessing to savor. The gift itself was tainted, but I could still appreciate how God could use the gift. It was hard to see the girls process seeing their dad become a cliché of a middle-aged man in crisis. And unfortunately, it was one of many steps of letting them process in their own way at their own pace.

It's hard to watch the people you love most hurt and not be able to do anything practical to fix it. But there was still a lot I could do. I could respect their journeys and relationships. I could walk with them at their pace, being willing to listen to their words and non-words. I could have uncomfortable conversations because it's what they needed, and I could answer questions as honestly as possible with the information I had.

My daughters' experiences are their own to share in their own way and in their own time. When you go through a crisis as a parent, no matter what ages your kids are, keep in contact with them and get to know them over and over as they grow and change. Notice how they're dealing with things and take cues from them. You can refuse to keep them in a box of your own comfort and expectations, assuming you know how they'll receive and process everything. Listen well and be ready when they are. Know that healing might take a lot of time but time itself doesn't heal. Humility, honesty, and availability are paramount to the healing process.

Being around family can be difficult but soothing, and family changes. I lost most of my ex's family. I tried to stay connected, but I don't think they knew how to stay engaged without feeling as if they were betraying him. It makes a difference whether a family is accustomed to talking about issues or sweeping them under the rug. Either can become an extreme in which people get hurt, whether there is too much confrontation that doesn't resolve things or not enough honest conversations which results in avoiding truth. There is a balance. We need to ask tough questions, so we can walk the journey alongside someone with truth. Without truth, we become more harmful than helpful to the person and our relationships.

My family loved me well. We had honest conversations. They gave me space. They helped in practical ways. They were available. Most of them didn't avoid the tough stuff.

My uncle died a little more than a month after my ex announced the end of the marriage. I had just moved out of the house I had shared with my ex. I was settling in without him, but I knew he was spending the weekend at his girlfriend's house, and I was struggling. I needed to be with others, so I decided to hang out with family at my aunt's house. We could struggle and be sad together with a variety of reasons. I sometimes suggest to people who are sad and hurting to watch a movie that might spur some tears, because they can basically cry all they want and blame the movie. I had enough stuff bothering me that weekend that I could cry and no one really knew why. I'm not even sure I knew why some of the time.

My uncle's services were several weeks later, and it was the first time I was around so many friends and family at the same time. I didn't realize how hard it would hit me. Many of the same people had been at my dad's services a little over a year earlier. Since my parents and aunt and uncle had so many memories together, many of the photos and memories involved my mom and dad, too, as well as other couples they'd hung out with for years.

I realized I'd never have that type of memorial service. At the end of my life, I wouldn't have the photos of memories with my life partner, because he wasn't in that role any longer. When someone dies, those moments and the relationship stay intact most of the time. We still speak fondly of the person who is missing. But that wouldn't be the case with me. The person I was grieving had left my life. He had cut himself out of my life and wanted no contact. He had removed himself from my family, people who had loved him well for many years. And at the end of my life, he wouldn't be there. The photos of the fun things we'd done wouldn't be there because of his choice to walk away and erase himself from any connection to me.

That realization was another wave of grief for me. We had a lot of fun together. We made a lot of memories together. And suddenly, because he wanted another life, I was pushed aside and severed from his life. I grieved the unfulfilled future of more memories with him, retiring and traveling together, having adventures with our grandkids together. I grieved no longer having the "together."

Sometimes when there is a major life transition, there's an opportunity to work through some of its effects and resolve it with others the best you can. But there are other life transitions, like the one I was experiencing, when someone chooses to be gone. Resolution with my ex wasn't an option. He wasn't open to conversation or honesty. So, working through stuff was mainly internal for me. Resolution and healing were still possible. They just looked and felt very different than other experiences I'd had with grief.

The weekend of the services for my uncle was difficult for me. After sharing a relaxing, fun dinner with family, I drove home to get a quick night's sleep before the next morning's service. My ex had rarely been enthusiastic about family gatherings, but there is a difference between being alone at a family event because someone chooses not to be there versus someone choosing not to be a part of the family ever again.

Grief overwhelmed me on the drive home that night. I sobbed and cried out to God and don't remember much of the drive. I was exhausted when I got home. I thought about the many things I knew people were going through, and I was grateful my grief was different. Yet some of my family members' faces as they processed my ex being gone kept flashing in my mind. I vented as I typed a short note, "Decent people don't do what he did. Refusing to consider another perspective, an invitation to process, an acknowledgment of hurt, enough respect for someone who lived and loved together for 27 years."

I prayed and cried some more. Then I started to get ready for bed. I reached into my pocket and found a Cheerio. I had been playing with my cousin's daughter and keeping her occupied with Cheerios and one ended up in my pocket. I smiled. It was as if God reminded me of the juxtapositions we experience in life. A family member had died, yet another young one was just starting her life. There is hope and anticipation of what the future holds.

I had a lot of hope and future ahead of me, too.

As I look back over the brief notes I wrote through that season, there is anguish and pain, but there is also hope and claims of truth.

- Love has no exception clause.

- I will pour everything out to God and trust Him, living the life ahead of me today, going through the motions, looking for opportunities to serve, recognizing blessings.

- It is not about me. It feels like it is about me. It is hard to get outside of my pain but I look around. How can I help others even when I feel unhelpable? With God's help, I can and I will.

- We see young love as foolish and risky but it is that act of faith to trust and build with someone else that reveals and builds faith.

- Are the people we want to die with the ones we are willing to live with? Sometimes we disconnect the two, but they are extensions of the same.

- Let a bruised heart, mind, and soul mend. It is tender.

- Sometimes things are said in crises that should not be held onto but looked at in the context of more time.

- I want to love and trust God so much that I have no problem letting go of what He's temporarily given to me to care for and love.

- My strength, courage, and identity comes from God. Before this and still. The core of me has not changed. I am asking God to refine me, taking away the unnecessary and strengthening the essential.

18

Declaring truths is important, whether you're in a crisis or not. It is only when you know truth that you can filter what comes in as something to accept or set aside.

Because of the many horrible things my ex said throughout the process, I knew I needed distance for my emotional safety and spiritual health. It should have been fairly easy to have limited contact because he didn't want contact. But of course, there were details to work through. It seemed smarter to let the attorneys deal with the details because it was too painful for me to only have financial conversations with the person I had done everyday life with for over two and a half decades. It just felt cold and demeaning to suddenly cut everything out of our lives except for numerical values and totals and possessions.

In practice, I kept contact limited, but it wasn't easy for many months. I still felt very connected to him. He had been clear about what he wanted (and didn't want), but I still cared. I knew he was rejecting and ignoring many people and relationships, lashing out at others, and it hurt me to imagine the pain he might be causing himself and others. I knew there were consequences to his choices, but I still had hope that he would make different choices with more respect for himself and others.

My heart was still very tender toward him. But I listened to God setting up healthy boundaries for me. I only engaged in conversation when I felt at peace doing so. I hadn't seen him since mediation, which was an option quickly taken off the table. Several months into the divorce process, his attorney hadn't responded to a proposed settlement request. I stopped by his house to find out how soon he would sign but stayed in the van with a plan to be able to leave quickly if needed. We had a brief conversation, and he said he'd sign the settlement as long as I would switch and give him the more reliable vehicle. (I agreed, but that was the first of several "I'll sign if..." agreements that fell through.)

At some point in the brief conversation, I mentioned I prayed for him often.

Of course you do. You're still drinking the Kool-Aid.

Ouch. Although, it didn't hurt me as much as I felt it hurt him.

That was enough of a reality check for me. He wasn't in a place to receive my care or extend respect and compassion. I would drive away and see if God had another opportunity planned in the future.

A couple months later, I took a trip. Friends decided I needed to take a break and get out of town. They worked together, and one paid for my flight, and the other hosted me in Colorado. I still tear up at the generosity. That trip was healing to me. I had a lot of time to hike and cry and pray. Plus, I got to make so many more memories with one of my best friends.

My friend took me into the mountains to a small town she had visited often when she was growing up. It had natural hot springs, and we soaked and talked and relaxed. We went to vapor caves. I couldn't stand the temperatures as long as she could, but it was still a purifying experience for me.

The air was stifling. I was sweating. And then the toxins seemed to begin to pour out of me. Tears fell, and I reminded myself to breathe. I fell into a rhythm of deep breaths in and out, and as I breathed I prayed.

I had noticed on the trip that any time I focused on my ex for too long, I felt toxic. Any time I focused on God, even for a short time, I had hope. The pain was still there regardless but it had context and purpose when I filtered it through God.

Often when I am struggling and pray, especially when I can't find the words to say, I keep it super simple and pray with the breaths. As I exhale, I commit to getting rid of my preferences and struggles, anything God wants to prune from me. With the exhale, I try to give more of myself to Him. When I breathe in, I commit to letting Him fill me, equipping me with truth and challenging me to trust Him.

As I sat in the vapor cave, some of the toxic things my ex had said to me bubbled up, and the tears flowed. But as I breathed, I let God truth check and release the lies. I didn't believe them, but I also hadn't let go of some of them. I was hanging onto the hurt they caused. I needed God to replace them with His truth.

You aren't enough. I deserve more.

You are enough. Keep growing, keep learning, keep searching.

We have never been compatible.

No one gets to redefine the truth of the past.

Quit crying and get over it.

Cry when you need to, then move forward. Healing will be a long process.

You will never be as mature as me.

Maturity is not age-related. Character is always revealing.

You have never really known me.

People get defensive when you are close to them. Love them anyway.

I feel sorry for you if you thought I was your best friend.

His rejection is not as powerful as my acceptance.

Breathe out. Breathe in.

I continued to pray for many minutes. I was soaked in sweat and tears, but when I lifted my head and walked up the narrow steps, I was cleaner, lighter, freer.

There were more opportunities for me to love my ex well in the months that followed. Of course, I could pray at any time. I could help by speaking to others about him in honest but non-disparaging ways when they asked.

And then I got an email out of the blue from my ex asking me to pause the divorce process. It was tough to know the boundaries through that brief season. I didn't sense that he wanted to reconcile. His breakup with his girlfriend must have rattled him enough that he needed to talk it through with someone. I felt for him but didn't want to trust he was in a healthy place. I walked and prayed nearby when I knew he had an appointment to talk to someone. I sat in on a future appointment so he could share what he felt like he needed to say in order to move forward. I tried to encourage him once again to be honest with himself and get healthy for his benefit and for people who loved him. I offered a hug and he accepted it. We even took a few walks together.

I tried to encourage him the best I could. I looked for hints of regret. I listened for clues of apologies and hopes for the future. There were some nice moments of casual conversation and glimpses of honesty. But I also heard deep rationalization and deflection.

.....

I jotted a note in my app:

I got an email about wanting to pause the process and it makes me wonder...am I being manipulated? Does he even know what he wants or is he just afraid of not "winning" and getting what he wants out of the divorce? I truly want him to be healthy, but I need to be healthy, too. I need to be compassionate and wise. I want to believe and hope for the best, but what exactly is that? This process of a divorce is hard, but trying to work through all the hurt? Wow. That's hard, too. Because now we have all the things that he says led up to him leaving (and I'm not even sure he grasps what all that truly is) plus all the hurt of his harshness, betrayal, deceit, and meanness. It's a lot to take in. But honestly? I have peace with pursuing the divorce. Of course, I want him to pursue counseling. Of course, I want him to be the best person he can be for the girls, his family, his friends, and his future. But that doesn't involve me. He made it very clear he doesn't want me in his life, that there was no wiggle room in negotiating. He made that break severe and irrevocable. Can God redeem anything? Absolutely. But is this one of those things He will redeem? Perhaps not in the way I originally wanted, but He will certainly redeem me (and others) through the process.

.....

It was a brief season of occasional contact, perhaps a month, and I would do it again. But through it, I was keenly aware of my vulnerabilities. I knew my heart was still soft toward him, because God had kept it that way. In the time that had passed, God had strengthened me and set solid boundaries, and I knew I could trust Him to guide me, equip me, and warn me. Any time I would set a time to walk with my ex, close friends knew where I was and were praying for both of us.

I was thankful for the experience of having a few conversations. I was also thankful for the clarity the conversations revealed as I listened closely to things he said.

Could we still be friends but agree to not have to talk through all that happened?

Could we get a divorce but then live together?

Could you just give me a little bit more in the settlement?

I had a peace about every walk except the last one. Of course, I didn't know it was the last one at the time, but it was obvious something needed to change. I was glad he was processing aloud, but he didn't respect me enough to be honest or listen well. So, I said we needed to move forward and we couldn't move forward in two directions at once. He immediately responded that he had decided months earlier to get a divorce and that hadn't changed. Then he switched the conversation to finances and the settlement, and I felt as if I couldn't breathe again.

It was heart-wrenching and clarifying. I drove to the church and sat by myself in the dark worship center and sobbed. Hearing he wanted a divorce this time wasn't as explosive as the first time. It didn't catch me off guard. It still hurt. I still wished it could be different. But based on the limited contact we had, it didn't surprise me. I would have been more shocked had he been humble and said he was sorry and wanted to try to salvage our relationship. It's a shock I would have welcomed, because although I knew reconciling would have been difficult, I knew nothing was impossible.

Instead I sat in the dark and grieved again. I was sorry he was where he was, and I was sorry for the fractures that would continue to ripple through lives because of his choices. But I was thankful, too. Thankful for God's guidance and provision. For Him opening my eyes to see truth and for keeping my heart soft. For the people He'd surrounded me with and the challenges He was growing me through.

I prayed, and I walked into the darkness of the night air with hope.

I went home and ate a giant cupcake from my favorite cupcakery. I had bought it earlier in the day. Many months earlier, someone who had gone through something similar had told me I wouldn't eat for a while then

95

would eat an entire pie or something at some point. As I ate the cupcake, I thought of those words. It took me longer than she projected, and it wasn't too excessive, but for me, it was a lot, and it seemed to reset something in me. I chuckled through the tears and a late night sugar rush.

I took a deep breath.

19

After listening to a teaching several years ago, I bought an oversize pillow that boldly declared PRAY BIG. It was a constant reminder of so many biblical examples of bold, big prayers. The pillow was in my home office until my ex and I had moved into our new home several months before our marriage ended. When we moved, the pillow found a new home on our bed. On most days, I was reminded to pray big at least twice.

The night my ex announced he wanted a divorce, I moved into the guest room. The PRAY BIG pillow stayed in his room. But when I walked by or in the room during those several weeks before I moved, the pillow was nearly always face down on a chair or the floor. Even if the bed had been made, that one pillow remained tossed aside. I intentionally placed it on the bed a few times, and each time, it was face down on the other side of the room the next day.

When I moved out of the house, PRAY BIG went with me in more ways than one. It was one of the first things I saw each time I walked into my safehouse. Praying big has become a way of life for me, planted years ago by a simple Bible teaching. Its simplicity strengthens me. It humbles and emboldens me to consistently pray big.

Prayer has been monumental in helping me through the fractured into wholeness process. Prayer has been my foundation, encouragement, and accountability. It has nourished and challenged me. As disoriented as I was in those early days with the swirling pieces piercing me, I leaned hard into God and communicated with Him more than anyone else, including myself. My self-talk regularly morphed into God-talk. He was listening anyway, and if I just talked to myself, what insight would I gain? How long would I spin? How far off track would I get?

Leaning so closely into God was comforting and stabilizing. I still wasn't comfortable, and I rarely felt stable, but sometimes we have to accept a glimpse of truth over our feelings and experiences.

Prayer filled the gaps of every day and seeped into spaces I didn't know existed. I had to intentionally breath as I walked, prayed, and sat with my thoughts swirling. And sometimes those prayers were as simple as, "God, I have no idea...but you do." Over and over, I declared my trust in Him. It was an act of submission and obedience, but it also served as a reminder for me. A reminder that I always have a choice to trust Him or not, to seek His way or mine. It seemed that every moment that wasn't filled with some activity was instantly filled with a deep desire to check in with God.

Sometimes I screamed out to Him. Sometimes I wept with Him. I tried always to express my gratitude, because even in the depths, I could find something to be grateful for. At times, I was thankful for being alive. Other times, I wasn't. But I could be thankful for others and their lives and their lives' impact on mine. I often prayed for others. God led me through webs of people, connecting how one need connects with another. I think those are some of my favorite moments of prayer. They feel like long walks with friends. Even when my prayers involve heavy burdens others are carrying, handing them over to God and walking alongside them seems to highlight the rays of light piercing the clouds.

The accountability God gifted me through prayer always strengthened me. He is so patient to let me vent, yet He also seems to know when to prompt me to stop spinning. One of my daughters often walked around the kitchen table while talking on the phone. Watching her made me dizzy, but I get it. It's how I feel when I pray sometimes. I need to move, but I keep going in a circle, and God lets me spin and spin and spin, almost like a spider spins and weaves together a web. Sometimes, I felt like I'd get to a point when God would say, "Time to stop. If you don't, you're going to weave yourself right into this web and get stuck."

He was simply prompting me to set the boundaries He knew were best and to trust Him with the next steps. I wasn't going to figure it out. He wasn't going to give me sudden and complete understanding of it all. But I could trust Him. He is constant. He is invested.

Sometimes I felt such a need to pray, I knew to not pray would be disobedient. I wouldn't completely understand the purpose behind the prompt to pray, because I didn't always have a specific motivation or need, but sometimes our response is more about obedience than pursuit of an outcome. We are often results-oriented when God wants us to be relationship-oriented.

Prayer isn't just about asking for something. No relationship works when all we do is ask for stuff. God wants it all from us—the questions, doubts, exclamations, thankfulness, confusion, anger, and everything else. He doesn't want it to be a continual vent session, where we just spew on Him (although that is okay from time to time). He wants us to share life with Him. After all, He shares life with us; He created life for us. We are the life He created. At least part of it. Sure, He knows what's going on with us, but don't you appreciate when people share with you and include you in their process?

Obviously, God doesn't need us to fulfill a need in Him, but that's what makes it even better. He longs for us to savor life with Him. He doesn't need us, but He wants us. And that kind of relationship is amazing. It's unconditional, yet it includes boundaries and accountability. Likewise, prayer is amazingly freeing, yet it has secure and comforting boundaries.

My prayer life, while already rich, deepened and soared. I saw my interactions with God from a broader perspective. I let Him seep into every bit of my schedule and thought life. He listened to it all. He kept it all in check. He reassured me and straightened me out. He directed me and provided for me. He constantly nudged me out of my comfort zone, but the trust that developed through those nudges secured my steps, my actions, and my attitudes.

While I felt as if I was in nearly constant communication with God, there were also times I felt Him drawing me to pray in specific ways or for particular people with such strength I nearly had no choice. Sure, I know I still had a choice, but He can be very persuasive. Sometimes He had me pray in a certain place or position, but most of the time, the focus was on a specific person. It could be people I knew were going through challenges, or people I had no idea what was going on in their lives. It was sometimes far-reaching people I knew were impacted by the ripple effects of the divorce. And many times it was for my ex.

No matter my difficulties with him, no matter how much he hurt me, I cared. Not in the sense of needing him to love me or apologize or make amends. As time passed, it really had little to do with me. I was out of the equation as far as he was concerned, but he was still cared for and loved. Even if he couldn't accept it, I prayed for God to extend His hand of generous grace. I prayed not in spite of what my ex had done and continued to do but because of who God is and will always be.

Sometimes it was easy to pray. Words flowed from my heart as tears often flowed down my cheeks. Other times the words shot out of my mouth with a strength I hardly recognized. Most of the time, it was not my own strength. Praying with such boldness was daunting, but it was right. Still other times, I had no words, and I would simply say something like, "God, I have no idea. I don't know. But you do. I trust you."

I didn't pray to get a specific result, because to be honest, I didn't know what that specific result should be. Only God knew exactly what was needed each time I prayed. My response was to pray and trust. God's job was to do the heavy lifting.

Not everyone prays. I get that. It was crucial for me, but you might be in a different place. I don't know what you're going through, but I encourage you to do something to put one foot in front of the other. Perhaps one of these ideas will help you take one step forward.

• Get out of bed. Seriously: there will be some days that if this is all you accomplish, count it a success.

• Get dressed. For those days when getting out of bed seems like a huge success, getting dressed makes you a rock star.

• Pray for others. It might feel like you're the only one in pain, but reminding yourself of other needs, even if they seem minuscule compared to yours, and being willing to pray about them will help your perspective.

- Be intentional about healing. It's a process. Do one thing each day that sets you up for healing.
- Stop destructive behaviors. It's easier said than done when you're in a crisis, but certainly don't add anything to your habits that you'll have to undo later. You'll have enough baggage. Don't unnecessarily add more.
- Reach out to someone, ideally someone who doesn't rubber stamp everything you say. You need people who will speak the truth to you, and you need to listen.
- Honor God. Whatever that looks like in your situation. He might prompt you to do something that is not your first choice. It might be difficult. But you won't regret doing the best thing each step of the way, regardless of how difficult it is.

20

Something else I did often was walk. Walking has pretty much always been soothing to me. When I still lived with my parents, I'd take long walks up the country road or the field road to enjoy the view of farmlands. I found peace in the midst of nature. Once I was married and had small girls, we walked to the library and park. I walked with them in the stroller so much that I had to get replacement tires.

There was something grounding about walking. I wasn't much of a jogger. When I was walking, I could think and pray and process. Jogging always took too much effort for me. I didn't like the process of making sure my strides were aligned and so on. I just wanted to get into the zone and walk, breathing in fresh air and clearing my mind.

I trained for a marathon once. It was time-consuming. I'm glad I did it...once. When I reached the finish line, my dad asked when I planned my next one. "Um, never." But I've been considering it again...

I had gotten out of the habit of walking the preceding couple of years, but I'd walked several times when I was away on the retreat just before my ex's announcement. I felt as if I had already taken a few steps into a healthier routine. Why not continue? But in those early days of the exploding pieces of my marriage, I was doing great just to put one foot in front of the other. But I pressed on because I knew it was good for me. Especially when I still lived in the house with my ex, walking gave me space away.

Sometimes I walked in silence, savoring the stillness around me. Much of the time, I blared worship music. Sometimes I walked to and around the park. When I had large blocks of time, I drove to my favorite long trail in a nearby town. It had been built on an old railroad track and was a gorgeous straight trail that included an overhead canopy of arching tree limbs and several scenic bridges. Sometimes I would walk until I had a sense of calm. There were times it would take hours, but in the end, I'd be physically exhausted yet emotionally and spiritually recharged and clear.

As I walked, I often cried. Much of the time, tears ran silently down my cheeks. After more than one walk, my face nearly felt raw. I felt empty yet full as I poured myself and my hurts and fears out and let God fill me with his strength and reassurance. More than once, I ran into someone I knew. Most of the time, I would sniffle and smile and assure people I'd be okay but just had a lot of wrestling and healing to do. There were a couple times when I couldn't catch my breath when I'd start to talk to someone. Fortunately, that only happened with people who, for one reason or another, understood and gave me compassion and space.

My local park walk became somewhat routine, and that routine provided stability. I got stronger as I walked. Putting one foot in front of another up and down hills was the physical exercise of what I was choosing to do emotionally and spiritually. One step. One reach. One effort. Then another and another.

As I walked, I ran into old friends and met new friends during those early months. People who saw me on a regular basis provided encouragement and company. I was constantly reminded of people's goodness and generous kindness.

A man who worked part-time in the park watched out for me (and others) when we walked at night. He parked where he could see walkers at multiple points, and he knew how long it should take each of us to reach those points. If we were delayed by much, he'd drive the route and check on us. When I didn't wear bright or reflective clothes, I got scolded, because it was more difficult for him to see me. I didn't mind the reminder. People who engage and encourage aren't necessarily intrusive. People care.

I've always enjoyed walking in the light rain. During those early months, I was nearly always crying while walking anyway, so the rain and tears mixed. But every now and then I got caught in a downpour or storm.

One morning, my pup and I walked to the park and got stuck in a drenching rain. I snapped a photo and later posted:

The rain came earlier than I expected. I was quickly drenched. Della didn't mind. As we sat in the park shelter, I listened to the beautiful rain and felt the mist as the wind blew under the roof. Perhaps today, on Good Friday, on the eve of the first major holiday since my family was surprisingly, abruptly altered, I especially needed this sudden rain. Rain cleanses, pounds, erodes, stings, nourishes. God provides through it all. And I will walk in it. With him.

My ex later scolded me for posting something that would prompt people to contact him and ask him what was going on. Sometimes accountability is unwelcome because the truth is hard to admit even when we think we are confident in what we're doing.

I also got stuck in a storm while on my long railroad trail, where it is a bit more difficult to find shelter. I was about a mile from one end (the opposite end as my vehicle) when the wind roared and sent twigs and small debris flying. I stood still for a moment, trying to decide what to do. Should I take cover in the ditch? I didn't feel as if I had the luxury of taking time to check the radar or call someone. I decided to run. That mile seemed long. A couple large branches dropped behind me, than another dropped in front of me. I climbed over it and continued. I prayed as I ran in limited visibility. Yet a calmness washed over me as the rain drenched me to the skin. If something happened to me in the storm, I had contentment that I was in one of my happy places. If nothing happened, I had a good story to tell, not to mention getting to splash in the rain.

I thought of one of my first dates with my ex, when I had shocked him by splashing in a puddle as we walked around the zoo. I liked adventure. He liked tidy. We later got caught in the rain and escaped into the elephant house with our orange sherbet cones. After we left the zoo we ate at a nice Italian restaurant, with our damp clothes and hair. To me, it was a way to enjoy each other's company while letting down our guard.

Even in the middle of that storm on my favorite trail, not knowing if a large limb would fall on me at any moment, I smiled at the memory of that day at the zoo and jumping in the puddle. My ex had looked at me, appalled at my spontaneity. Through the years, I had splashed for fun with him and trudged through storms with him. And I would have trudged through more. But this storm race was on my own. And it was okay. I was okay.

I reached the end of the trail and took shelter—sort of. The wind seemed to be weakening a bit, and I was so drenched that another drop of rain would not make a difference. A man came racing under the shelter on his bike. He had missed most of the storm. We checked out the radar and talked about options. I had a five mile hike back to my car. Once I knew the storm had mostly passed, I struck back out on the trail. Sure, it was still raining, but it didn't make a difference to me. As I made my way over and around the limbs scattered across the trail, I began to thank God.

My gratitude began to circle wider and wider. I continued to walk and thank God for the storms of my life—not just the protection from them but for the storms themselves. For the debris that was cleared. For the drenching rain that refreshed me. For the journey itself.

I don't remember much else about that walk to my car. It went by so much faster than I would expect. My feet squished in my shoes but I felt light and airy. I felt renewed.

That is what gratitude does.

WHOLENESS

21

Forgiveness doesn't change the need for safety and health, for boundaries and guidelines, but it loosens the binding on my heart. It gives me freedom and peace and the ability to not return to a situation of hurt but to move forward in healing. It is a vulnerability not to the person who betrayed and belittled me but a vulnerability to God who will prune me, mold me, comfort me, and challenge me.

Forgiveness is an oddity. It seems to go in so many directions. It feels freeing yet oppressive, reorienting yet unsettling, self-beneficial yet selfless. What is it exactly? Why does it seem so simple and complete at times yet resurfaces at the most alarming times?

We sometimes approach forgiveness like a beach ball in the pool. We throw our body on top of to try to make it sink in a pool. It refuses to be held under. Forgiveness is not hiding or shoving or disguising anything. It is truthful, authentic, and revealing.

And forgiveness is a process.

Maybe we think it's a one-and-done thing because we think God's forgiveness looks like that. But does it, really? Sure, the act of Jesus dying on the cross for the forgiveness of our sins, our junk, our rejection of Him, was a point-in-time action but be careful projecting onto Him. First, He is God. His ability to forgive is going to be a bit better than ours. Second, even God's forgiveness is a process. He can forgive all in an instant, but He forgives as we yield. We have to be willing in order to receive God's forgiveness.

Forgiveness comes easier at some times and in some situations than others. It's not predictable. We can forgive and move on from a significant offense yet feel stuck on something minor. We don't struggle with the same unforgiveness as others. We all move through hurt and betrayal in different ways and timing. Sometimes, we aren't even aware of some of the bitterness that takes root and grows within us.

Forgiveness is like healing and redemption: it is a process. Forgiveness is entwined with healing and redemption and is nearly always part of being fractured into wholeness.

We often want to highlight the personal benefits forgiveness has for us:

- To forgive is to set a prisoner free and discover that prisoner is you.
- The first to forgive is the strongest.
- Forgive not because the other person deserves forgiveness but because you deserve peace.
- Forgiveness is the attribute of the strong.
- Unforgiveness is like drinking poison and expecting the other person to die.
- Forgiveness doesn't excuse the other person's behavior but prevents their behavior from destroying your heart.

True forgiveness cannot be conditional. My forgiveness does not depend on my ex's apology, behavior, or response. If it did, I would still be waiting, hanging onto burdensome weight and bitterness. The choice of forgiveness is deeply personal and generously sacrificial. Forgiveness is an ongoing attitude, like kindness, compassion, and patience. As the attitude invades our thoughts, it seeps out through our actions. Forgiveness in its purest form—and as God intends and models—is something we carry into each moment not simply something we grant after an offense.

The Bible says God will forgive us as we forgive others, but forgiving with the goal of getting God's forgiveness in return is narrow-minded. It is similar to doing good with the primary goal of storing up treasures in heaven, to which the Bible also refers but does not set as the ultimate goal for doing good.

Forgiveness is a gift—an underserved gift—that has far reaching blessings among people and within our hearts, minds, and souls. Forgiveness is like wind—difficult to see but impossible not to feel.

Forgiveness is redemptive love. It is grace in practice. Forgiveness doesn't change the past but it does broaden the future. Forgiveness helps us move forward and grow, looping back to heal and reconcile what will be valued in our future while also letting go of what needs to stay in the past. Forgiveness doesn't forget everything but, as we trust God to filter, we remember the truths that challenge and refine us, and we lay aside what God declares as out-of-season. When we keep what wasn't intended for a new season, we invite rot to infect even the most beautiful things in our lives.

I watched the effects of this very thing. I was a casualty. When my ex allowed what was rotting in his life to sit in the darkness for too long without attending to it, the stench became too much. The only response seemed to be to throw out much more than the core culprits. And he lost some beautiful people and relationships in the purging process.

Reflecting on the journey up to this point, I cannot separate forgiveness and redemption. God has used every step of forgiveness as redemption. He challenged me to forgive when I wanted to hang on a little longer. He spurred me to put out feelers of repair and reconciliation and blessed me with clear answers in return. He revealed bits and pieces of what small things I was clenching in my fist. Most importantly, He taught me how to trust Him for forgiveness, and He took me deeper in our relationship. Forgiveness, healing, and redemption revealed God's character to me and made me more authentic—because the more completely we know God, the more authentically we become who He created us to become.

22

Grief is a journey, and it can involve many types of loss.

Grief happens before an actual loss, through the loss, and long after the loss.

Grief is intimately tied to forgiveness and redemption.

Grief takes time.

My life has felt inundated and weighted with grief over the past several years.

I had said goodbye to my dad a year before my husband left. I dealt with the grief of my dad's death ahead of time, as I watched him walk through doctors' appointments, tests, and cancer treatments and trials. I savored the moments I had with him. Nothing was left unsaid. It was still devastating to lose him, to not be able to text or call him, but the way he, my mom, and those of us close to him faced it all gave me peace.

The loss of my husband and marriage has been a different grief. I didn't have opportunity to deal with it ahead of time, and there is still more that I don't understand than what I know. There was no processing with my ex—just rejection. It has been a grief difficult to grasp, and it's challenging to share with others.

But grief is often a complicated thing.

We sometimes see grief as the experience of a memorial service or family gathering or receiving line. But it is also in the everyday struggles and spaces. I paused during some of those moments to jot notes about my grief process.

.....

Today is just hard. I don't know why. I drove out of state to my nephew's game. All I wanted to do was come home. But I also didn't want to come home. Everything is a reminder of what I no longer have. And I

111

know I have so much. I am thankful. I really am, but I am simply deeply sad today. I know I have such a good, full future ahead, and that I don't need to fit into a mold to be content. In fact, the marriage mold is not one I even have any interest at all in fitting into right now. But I listen to others talk about their family plans and reminiscing memories. I have none of that. No anticipation of a future with the person I planned to spend the rest of my life with. No fulfillment of some of the dreams and plans we had. And I can't even really reminisce about the times we had, because it is all so tainted. While the girls are still my family, it is so fragmented. I am just so very tired and worn. I am trying to settle into God's presence and let Him comfort me and guide me, rebuild me. But sometimes I just want to quit.

…..

I hadn't cried since the beginning of the year - the new year I was glad to welcome, putting last year behind me. I hadn't cried since the reality check of having the script flipped yet again and him not settling as he said he would if only I would wait until the new year. But meeting with my friend and hearing her say she saw an older couple holding hands at the local Y and missing that for me. Yes, I will miss that, too. I cried not out of hurt or devastation but out of healing and contentment with where I am and where I might be. I not only will be okay, but I am okay. Then I teared up thinking about my ex's parents and family. I had said my goodbyes when it seemed clear they didn't want to stay in contact. It is difficult to be expendable. But I know they are uncomfortable and uncertain.

…..

Someone mentioned that I seem to be just fine without him. That I didn't "need" him. True. There are many things I don't need. I didn't need him. I wanted him. In some ways, that is more important. That is beyond dependency. It is desire. It is pursuit. It is choice. But options and choices change.

…..

It's different now. I was willing to fight for my marriage. But you can't fight very effectively when the other person runs from it, so my fight is

112

different now. Divorce so often feels like a fight against marriage, but that seems counterproductive to me. So I go through the necessities of the legal process but focus primarily on fighting for health and growth and healing. I'm sure sometimes that looks odd. I know many times it feels odd. I was so willing to fight not only for the marriage but for my husband, personally, and as the person I loved and wanted to spend the rest of my life with. But sometimes people are not willing to receive what we are willing to give. I grieve that opportunity to give and fight. I know people will see the worst in a person or relationship if that's what they want to see, and they'll see hope and possibilities if that's what they prefer to see. It is each person's choice, but that choice affects their perspective, and those choices have ripple effects, and many people grieve.

.....

A little over a month following my ex's announcement, I was at my mom's house. My dad's dog was still alive but had some health issues. We'd had her at the vet a couple times, and she seemed to improve a bit. But that day she wasn't doing well at all. We loaded her in the van and drove to the vet, who is a friend of mine. He came out of his office to the van and confirmed what we already thought. He gently carried her inside, and my mom and I followed. We stayed with her until she was gone.

I was fine until we walked outside. It all hit me. That dog had been through a lot with my dad, and she was gone. My dad was gone. The vet had been through his own family trauma recently, and his son was gone. My ex had been with me when we comforted him and his wife. My ex had comforted me when my dad died. My ex was gone now, too. Yes, in a different way, but it was all loss, and grief seemed to wrap around and fill me.

It just seemed too much in the moment.

There were many times when the grief of my marriage was deepened by my ex's abandonment. I was surrounded by people who loved me well. But someone I loved had walked out of my life without warning and without respect, without the consideration of the time we'd spent together, how I would respond, what I would need, or what he left in

113

his wake. I knew I wasn't the only one in the world who had ever been abandoned, but I felt alone at times.

The process of grief includes many moments of vulnerabilities. Those vulnerabilities open us up to a variety of experiences, both positive and negative, which can both be productive and invite us into growth.

I often worked through my struggles and grief process as I wrote.

.....

Perhaps that sweet, powerful weekend was to place me in a vulnerable and weak place, a good place to see my need for God's strength. I was close to tears all day. Just down. Then the dam broke. Part of it was standing in the office, so close to where I was the last time I had a real conversation with my ex. Who am I kidding? It wasn't a real conversation. But when we got home and he got so angry at me for wanting him to be honest with our family, when he blamed me for the hurt that was about to happen, when we had to go to the basement for a tornado warning and I was thankful to be able to separate myself from him and his hurt, when he went upstairs before me and I lagged behind to get my bearings, when I went upstairs and he said he thought it would be different. Then I continued to pack and prepare to move out a few days later. That night seems so long ago. But there I was in that office weeks later, praying over someone I respect, who is facing a different kind of trial and uncertainty. I needed a long peaceful walk, and I just couldn't stop crying. The wave of sadness washed over me, only this time it didn't drown me. It made me gasp. It made me flounder. But I also knew it was cleansing and wouldn't last for long. I got to pet a Great Dane pup and cry with a friend. Another friend insisted on coming to see me and brought much-needed tissues. This journey is so hard. But I am blessed along the way. Sadness can be healing. I've learned to walk through it, finding snippets of joy along the way, filling my bucket and heart as I collect them.

.....

Grief felt like so many things in my life. I once wondered,

Is God preparing me? Pruning me? Killing me? Healing me? Sometimes it all feels the same.

There were days and moments I was overwhelmed. There are others where I felt God was holding an umbrella over me.

Regardless of our feelings, like so much else in our lives, we have to yield grief to God in order to deal with it truthfully and healthily. As I grieved, God continued to remind me that the process was not focused on me getting my way but letting God have His way and joining Him along it. I didn't need to stress about what was done to me but focus on what God has done for me and what He can do to and through me. The point isn't to improve my life but to improve my Christ-likeness. Life isn't centered around me. Or you. When we begin to feel that way, we begin to believe everything we have belongs to us. We stress when interest rates go up because it impacts *our* finances. We stress when something interrupts us because it impacts *our* schedule. We even stress over whatever we think ebbs away at *our* spiritual lives.

I have learned that authentic grief gives way to authentic joy. Taking time to grieve is difficult, because the waves come and go and at times seem overwhelming. When the waves are not in sight, it is still sometimes hard to enjoy the moment, because experience reveals another wave will indeed come. But dealing with grief as healthily and honestly as we can matters. The pursuit through grief will never completely be in the past. But the pursuit can morph into undeniable growth. Could we get the same sort of growth without the grief? I doubt it.

Psalm 40 captures the transformation, not specifically through grief but through seeking and trusting God.

I waited patiently for the Lord,
and He turned to me and heard my cry for help.
He brought me up from a desolate pit,
out of the muddy clay,
and set my feet on a rock,
making my steps secure.
He put a new song in my mouth,
a hymn of praise to our God.
Many will see and fear
and put their trust in the Lord.

How happy is the man
who has put his trust in the Lord
and has not turned to the proud
or to those who run after lies!
Lord my God, You have done many things—
Your wonderful works and Your plans for us;
none can compare with You.
If I were to report and speak of them,
they are more than can be told.
You do not delight in sacrifice and offering;
You open my ears to listen.
You do not ask for a whole burnt offering or a sin offering.
Then I said, "See, I have come;
it is written about me in the volume of the scroll.
I delight to do Your will, my God;
Your instruction lives within me."
I proclaim righteousness in the great assembly;
see, I do not keep my mouth closed—
as You know, Lord.
I did not hide Your righteousness in my heart;
I spoke about Your faithfulness and salvation;
I did not conceal Your constant love and truth
from the great assembly.
Lord, do not withhold Your compassion from me;
Your constant love and truth will always guard me.
For troubles without number have surrounded me;
my sins have overtaken me; I am unable to see.
They are more than the hairs of my head,
and my courage leaves me.
Lord, be pleased to deliver me;
hurry to help me, Lord.
Let those who seek to take my life
be disgraced and confounded.
Let those who wish me harm

be driven back and humiliated.
Let those who say to me, "Aha, aha!"
be horrified because of their shame.
Let all who seek You rejoice and be glad in You;
let those who love Your salvation continually say,
"The Lord is great!"
I am afflicted and needy;
the Lord thinks of me.
You are my helper and my deliverer;
my God, do not delay.

Do not delay indeed, God.
In the meantime, I will seek and be glad.

23

As we deal with the blessings and challenges of life, we need to have integrity. There's a popular saying: "Integrity is what you do when no one is watching." I believe integrity is also what you do when anyone is watching. Integrity is leaning into wholeness and authenticity.

My ex and I often had conversations about integrity through the years. It was important to both of us. In a moment of transparency, he reflected on the impact his decision to handle leaving the marriage the way he did would have on his integrity.

I think we sometimes see integrity as how someone else perceives us. When we take that perspective, we don't see integrity with clarity. Integrity is a bend toward wholeness. There will always be a discrepancy, but the difference between where we are and what integrity in its completeness would look like within us is a space we always want to narrow. But we have to do so with humility and honesty.

I see a lot of selective integrity within people. We rationalize what is wrong that we want to see as right. Because we don't want to admit we are wrong, we challenge the concept of wrong itself. We question whether or not wrong actually exists. But we're usually willing to fight hard for the things we don't think are wrong that others project on us, while at the same time having very little patience for someone else's perspective and values.

Selective integrity justifies disrespecting others, then blames them for their response to your disrespect. As graphic as the illustration is, selective integrity justifies vomiting on others then wondering why they stink. Listen to the way you respond to people around you. It's easy to vomit on (or vent to if you prefer a more palatable visual) people you either know won't walk away from you or people you want to walk away from but don't care about leaving them whole and healthy.

But I find that vomiting on others always signifies some sort of illness, something not dealt with that spews from deep within. Selective integrity has that sickening effect. It hurts relationships and people.

Integrity should seek wholeness, not selection. It's not a convenience, what's comfortable in a specific situation. It doesn't change with the weather. It seeks and stands on truth. And truth doesn't change, but it does change us. Sometimes people want to find truth and claim it with an unwillingness to change. But we can't completely know truth. There is always more to reveal. We can glimpse it, but our comprehension is limited. As we seek it, we are changed by the journey. We yield, we doubt, we question, and we grow.

It's a fractured into wholeness journey.

Selective integrity is staying in the fracture. Integrity is healing into wholeness.

It's a space of grace.

I was reading my Bible one day and paused at Luke 4, which addresses the temptation of Jesus. I knew I had been in a wilderness on many levels. Unlike Jesus, I don't necessarily think the Holy Spirit led me there, but I know He was *with* me. Satan and I had some rough interactions. I was overwhelmed at times with his influence and impact. He is ugly and deceptive. He betrays and tricks. He minimizes and exaggerates. He rationalizes and excuses. He projects and pummels. But he doesn't have eternal power or authority. He doesn't get the last word. No matter what, I can still choose God. So can anyone else, no matter where they've been, what they've trusted from Satan, or how they've honored a false, deceptive authority in their life. Each of us can choose God no matter where we are. And we need Him no matter where we are— the wilderness or the mountaintop.

Choosing well no matter where we are or what we believe we want is integrity.

Integrity depends on our perspective, but it also keeps our perspective in check. After a vibrant exchange with someone on social media, I felt a bit oppressed. I realized some of it was because of a similar disregard and disrespect I had experienced at the end of my marriage. I took a step back and let God filter it. Soon I was overwhelmed by peace and the reminder to put on the full armor of God and trust Him. It's funny how in my distrust of someone who hurts me, I realize how much I trust the One who will not. My step was a little lighter for the rest of the day.

Integrity doesn't make everything feel good. Choosing well involves struggle. Sometimes it's misunderstood or unappreciated. Sometimes it's attacked. But another person's response doesn't define integrity. It's not that we shouldn't consider someone's response. We need to be respectful, and many times, we can learn a lot about ourselves, our values, and our behavior through our interactions with others. But we have to be willing to humbly consider what we can learn, be wise in the lessons, then be courageous in growing through them.

When my ex wondered how his choices would affect his integrity, I thought, "Doesn't every choice affect our integrity?" Every choice reveals our integrity, shining a bright light on it to highlight what needs to continue and highlight what needs to be eliminated. Integrity is the honesty to shine that light then be willing to change because of what we find.

24

During a particularly frustrating and exhausting time, a friend and I were texting. She was trying to lighten the mood and load a bit for me. Knowing I write a lot, she mentioned how the added complications I was experiencing in the divorce process might result in a good book someday. I responded, "Yes, either a good book or a mental institution."

Some of my humor along the way might have been borderline inappropriate.

As with anyone's journey, mine has a lot more details than I can (or should) share here. My main motivation for writing throughout my journey—whether it's here in book form or on my daily blog—is to share a story of redemption. It's not the complete journey. There is more healing and redemption to come, but this is a glimpse. As hard as it is at times, we need to share. It encourages others. It invites them into redemption.

A friend texted, "I wish you didn't have to go through this." I responded, "Me, too. Except that if it somehow honors God, I would prefer to go through it."

I can't tie my fractured into wholeness journey into a tidy bow. I probably never will. It's a knotted, frayed gathering of what remains of shredded threads. But it still binds. Redemption isn't only the completion of rebuilding. It is woven throughout the rebuilding process.

I appreciate the notes, comments, and spoken words of encouragement people have shared, letting me know my willingness to share has helped them. Sometimes an anonymous comment, message from an acquaintance, or affirmation from a close friend spurred me onward at just the right time. I experienced redemption from different angles—personally as well as in and through others.

And I know God has been redeeming people and situations I have little contact with now—not because I know details but because I know God's character. Even when it might not look as if redemption is part of the process, God has not stepped aside. People can walk away from and reject Him. But that doesn't mean He has stopped caring or pursuing. However, people might still decide to refuse Him. He is willing to leave the 99 to pursue the one who is lost and confused, disoriented, and in danger. But He doesn't always trudge away to pick up that solitary one. Sometimes He gives us space and patiently waits for us to make a decision and effort to return. The prodigal son left his home and demanded to take what was due him. His focus was on himself, his wants, his entitlement, and his happiness. He was sure being on his own was preferable to working through constraints and challenges at home.

While he was gone, his dad waited. He didn't follow him around, constantly trying to convince him of his wrong. He didn't cushion the impact of his choices. He let him face the consequences. He didn't sit in the muck with his son. He let his son get to a place where truth was right in front of him. He let his son walk home.

The son's steps might have been difficult, and I have no doubt the minutes and days passing at home for the father were hard, but they were filled with purpose and redemption. Even the days the son sat with the pigs had purpose and redemption in them.

We want to think redemption is simply the actual turn toward God, but it is so much more. When I sat in the dark bedroom that first night with the pieces of my life swirling around me and piercing my heart and soul, there was redemption. When I felt as if I stood on a precipice and was about to fall, there was redemption. When I looked into the cold emptiness of my life-love-and-partner and knew he was done, there was redemption. Not just for me but for him.

I loved my ex and I loved being married, but if my marriage is the cost of his redemption or someone else's, I offer it all for God to use. As life-altering as it is to me, the sacrifice is miniscule compared to God's sacrifice for me.

God is the focus. He is the purpose. He gets the glory.

People have told me I'm responding well, growing well, healing well. I appreciate the encouragement, but I don't want to be known for how I'm responding. I want God to be known for what He's done, what He's doing, and what we can trust Him to do in the future. The process of being fractured into wholeness is about Him. I'm the vessel, but He's the designer and molder.

It is our responsibility to respond to the process of redemption, but having a choice and having control are two different things. Redemption journeys look different. They don't always end in a specific snapshot of wholeness we prefer or expect.

I felt as if God was snipping the heart strings that tied me to my husband, just one or two at a time, like I was holding onto a bundle of beautiful helium balloons. God knew just how and when to cut those strings so that I could adjust. It still felt as if I was dropping to the ground over and over, but my feelings don't always accurately reflect a situation. With each snip, there was pain and adjustment.

Around the same time as my fracture, Lysa Terkeurst, author of *It's Not Supposed to Be This Way*, announced her fractured marriage. It looked like she and her husband were headed toward divorce. Lysa shared—authentically and appropriately—both relationship and personal struggles she and her husband had. She wrote, "A really great way to hurt the Kingdom of God here on earth is to take down Christian marriages." I agree. I believe I had one of the good marriages. Not perfect, but good, and for the majority of it, God-seeking. Lysa and her husband have since turned toward each other and God and are fighting for the marriage and faith. I continue to cheer them on through their redemption journey. Mine looks very different, yet they are both redemption journeys.

Instead of seeing redemption in a specific outcome or perceived wholeness, we need to become sensitive to seeing redemption in the fractures as well. Redemption is in the *into* of being fractured into wholeness.

The definition of redemption is "the action of saving or being saved from sin, error, or evil."

Sin might not be a popular word in our culture where we prefer to decide what is right and wrong and acceptable for each of us. Whatever word we use—sin, error, evil—circles back to what is at the root of it all, often summarized as "missing the mark."

I get that concept. After all, when we miss the mark, our momentum might be right, but the direction and aim throws us off. Our focus is not quite right. And the result is misplaced potential.

Why do we get so defensive about missing the mark, being told we could improve, or that there is actually a specific goal for us? We don't have a problem telling ourselves about our own goals or areas to improve. But if we're honest, we don't always have the most accurate, complete perspective of ourselves and what's all around us. We tend to focus on what we want to focus on and miss a lot of our surroundings in the process.

Why not welcome others into our lives, of course, filtering with truth and wisdom?

Finding the mark, focusing on it, missing it, resetting, and continuing that process is the redemption process. That is being fractured into wholeness.

At times, I haven't known the tools to use, the direction to face, or the advice to apply. I didn't have the strength or coordination. My eyes have been closed or filled with tears.

And all of that is part of the redemption process.

At times, I've loaded the bow and pointed the arrow with precision and focus. My strength and balance were steady and I was ready. I did not blink. And that is part of the redemption process, too.

25

The day my divorce was final, I gave my ex one more note, which I had written nearly a year and a half earlier, around the time I moved out of the house we had shared. I had left space for the end date, the death date of our marriage. I believe how we finish matters, perhaps even more than how we start.

No matter what happens, I want to finish well.

7/28/90-7/20/18

I never thought I would write a death date on the end of our marriage, but here we are. It is over. I will miss doing life with you. I see older couples walking or riding in a car, and I miss the memories we would have made as we grew older. I see grandparents walking into a restaurant or lifting kids into their car, and I miss the moments we would have laughed with our grandkids. I miss turning to you to listen to stories about your day. I miss asking for your help. I miss doing little things for you that you probably never noticed. But I know that you have chosen something and someone else, that you no longer want me in your present or future, and in time, I will work through the hurt and the grief and get through it. I love you too much not to forgive you and release you, as difficult as that is for me. There is absolutely nothing you could have revealed to me that I am confident I and we would not have been able to work through with time and effort, courage and humility. I am sorry you did not feel safe enough to do that. I will continue to pray that you face each day, decision, and challenge with integrity, courage, and honesty.

My fractured-into-wholeness journey isn't complete. Yours likely isn't either, because it's a process. Our lives are a process. I hope I've been encouraging to you, but I also hope I've challenged you. Not to do things the ways I have, not to process in the ways I have, but to step forward. To reflect on the past just long enough to gather the truth, and to begin to gently carry the pieces you need to heal toward wholeness.

I don't know if you've been hurt, or if you've done some hurting. Either way, forgiveness, healing, and redemption are all available to you. Struggle toward them.

Seek truth.

Wrestle with doubts.

Deal with consequences.

Reconcile with people.

Set healthy boundaries.

The end result might not look like you expect it to look, but the process will likely be clarifying and life-changing for you.

I hope you'll stay connected with me. Visit my blog for *Fractured Into Wholeness* encouragement sheets to print, post, and share. Subscribe to my blog for daily posts delivered to your inbox. Connect with me on Facebook, Instagram, and Twitter for daily encouragement and connections with others.

Let's do this thing together.

purepurpose.org

facebook.com/purepurpose

@purepurpose

@susanhlawrence

47615213R00075

Made in the USA
Middletown, DE
09 June 2019